T. Eaton

Canada's greatest store

Christmas Catalogue 1897

T. Eaton

Canada's greatest store
Christmas Catalogue 1897

ISBN/EAN: 9783741194375

Manufactured in Europe, USA, Canada, Australia, Japa

Cover: Foto ©Thomas Meinert / pixelio.de

Manufactured and distributed by brebook publishing software
(www.brebook.com)

T. Eaton

Canada's greatest store

THE GREATEST GOOD TO THE GREATEST NUMBER

MONEY REFUNDED IF GOODS
ARE NOT SATISFACTORY

CANADA'S GREATEST STORE

ALASKA

NORTH WEST
TERRITORY

DOMINION

BRITISH
COLUMBIA

ATHABASCA

KEEWATIN

NORTH EAST
TERRITORY

LABRADOR

ALBERTA SASKATCHEWAN

OF

ASSINIBOIA MANITOBA

CANADA

QUEBEC

ONTARIO

PACIFIC
OCEAN

TORONTO

ATLANTIC
OCEAN

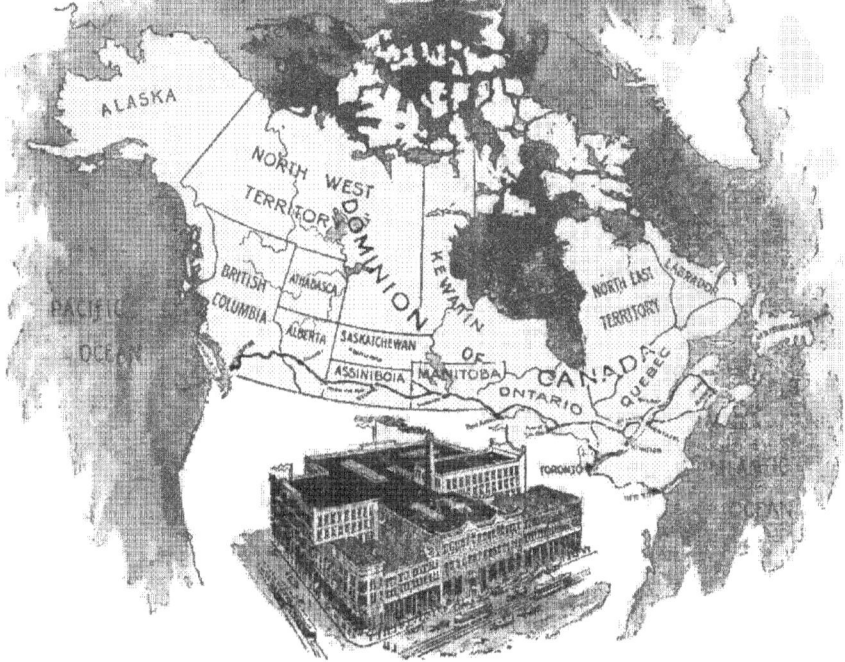

CHRISTMAS CATALOGUE 1897

THE T. EATON CO. LIMITED

190 YONGE ST.   TORONTO, ONT.

Holiday Goods

THIS STORE is full of Suggestions for Holiday Shoppers. Counters and shelves piled high with the best of everything from everywhere — altogether too many different things to touch upon here.

Toys, Dolls and Games
Fancy Toilet Articles
Glassware, China and Crockery
Knives and Scissors
Dress Goods and Silks
Jewelry and Cutlery
Pictures and Easels
Gloves and Handkerchiefs
Celluloid Novelties
Books and Stationery

Christmas Slippers and Shoes
Clothing of all sorts
Handsome Furs
Clocks and Silverware
Table Covers and Linens
Trunks and Valises
Umbrellas and Fans
Albums and Purses
All kinds of Furniture, Curtains and Rugs

Sensible and pretty things for the home. Gifts practical and dainty. Suitable Christmas Gifts in abundance.

CONSIDER THESE SUGGESTIONS.

If you don't find what you want in this Catalogue, refer to our FALL AND WINTER CATALOGUE NO. 39, where complete lines are fully represented.

ORDER EARLY WHILE ASSORTMENTS ARE COMPLETE.

Christmas Gifts.

STERLING SILVER.

A FEW SUGGESTIONS,

No. 1. Gents' military hair brushes, $6.00 pair.

No. 2. Ladies' hair brushes, $4.25, 5.25, 6.25 each.

No. 3. Ladies' hair comb, silver mounted, $1.00. $1.25.

No. 4. Cloth brush, $1.70, 4.25 each.

No. 5. Ladies' hat or bonnet duster, $1.50, 1.75, 2.00.

No. 6. Cut glass silver mounted vaseline holders, 1 inch diameter, 70c ; 1½ inch, 85c ; 2 inch, $1.30 ; 3 inch, $2.50. Puff box, cut glass, silver top, to match, $2.50.

No. 7. Nail polisher, 2½ inch, $1.25, 1.35.

No. 8. Gents' shaving brush, plain, beaded pattern, $1.90.

No. 9. Nail files, 20c, 40c, 60c, 80c, $1.00, according to size.

No. 10. Button hooks, 20c, 40c, 60c, 80c, $1.00.

No. 11. Curling tongs, silver handles, 6-inch, 75c ; 7-inch, 90c.

No. 12. Shoe horn, silver handle, 7-inch, $1.25.

No. 13. Sterling silver child's cup, $5.00, 5.50, 6.00 ; Louis XV. pattern, heavy, $8.25.

No. 14. Manicure scissors, 90c, $1.35, 1.50, according to size.

No. 14. Lace or embroidery scissors, 75c, $1.20, 1.40, 1.50, 1.60.

No. 14. Grape scissors, 5 inches long, $1.75. Remember all the silver parts of above articles are 925/1000 fine silver.

Articles mounted with sterling silver not illustrated but which we carry in stock—

Babies' hair brushes, silver handle, $1.25.

Hat markers, 40c.

Napkin rings, $1.00, 1.25, 1.50, 1.75.

Umbrella markers, 20c.

Satchel tags, 40c.

Collar button boxes, $3.50.

Bicycle tags, 40c, 65c.

Gents' mustache combs, 20c, 40c, 75c, $1.00.

Tie clasp, 25c.

For other lines of Sterling Silver Goods see Catalogue No. 37, page 147.

Emery strawberries, 40c, 50c, 75c.
Pocket knife, ladies', 65c, 90c.
Silver filigree thimble case, $1.90.
Cigar cutter (scissors), $1.25.
Ash trays and match holder, $2.25.
Pocket match safe, chased, $1.50 ; heavy plain,
$2.25.
Pocket stamp box, 75c.
Shaving stick in silver cases for gentlemen,
$3.25.
Silver bracelet, chain pattern, 75c, 90c, 1.20,
1.25, 1.50, 2.00.
Glove stretchers, $2.25.
Pumice stone, silver mounted, $2.00.
Pin cushions, on a silver stand, $1.00.
Pearl game counters, $1.00 per pair.
Tape measures, 75c, $1.00 each.
Seals for letters, 30c, 50c, 75c, $1.25.
3-piece manicure sets (nail file, button hook and
cuticle knife), 60c.
Gentlemen's suspenders, silver mounted, white,
light blue or black silk, $2.90.
Ladies' garters, silver buckle $1.50, 2.00 pair.
Ladies' companion set (scissors, thimble and
emery), $1.60.

Sterling Silver Flatware.

In satin-lined cases, half a dozen in case.
Coffeespoons, gold-lined bowl, $1.75.
Coffeespoons, heavy, silver bowl, $2.60 ; gold
bowl, $3.60.
Teaspoons, small size, $3.00 ; medium weight,
$4.00 ; heavy weight, $4.85 ; extra heavy,
$5.25.
Dessert spoons, full weight, $10.50.
Dessert forks, full weight, $10.15.

Black Enamelled Iron Clock.

8-day ½-hour
strike on a
cathedral gong,
4½-inch dial,
height 13½ in.,
width, 10¼ in.,
with white dial,
$9.80 ; perforated gilt dial,
$9.80 ; ivory,
porcelain and
giltdial, $10.80.
All our clocks
are tested before
shipping. For
other patterns
see our Fall and
Winter Catalogue for 1897-98.

Three New Rings for Christmas.

(Ladies' Rings.)

A10.

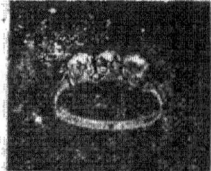

A20.

A30.

For other
patterns s e
our 1897 Fall
and Winter
Catalogue, No.
39, page 132.

A10 14k Solid gold real diamond ring, a special,
$10.00
A20 10k Solid gold ring, 3 real fire opals, a
special, $4.00.
A20 14k Solid gold ring, 3 real fire opals, a
special, $4.85.
A30 10k Solid gold ring, 5 real fire opals, a
special, $5.00.
A30 14k Solid gold ring, 5 real fire opals, a
special $6.00.

Pocket Knives.

No. 1. Gents' pocket knives, two blades, buffalo, stag or bone handles, 25c ; pearl handles,
35c, 50c.
No. 2. Gents' pocket knives, three blades,
pearl handle, bolstered or tipped ends, 75c,
$1.00, 1.25.
No. 3. Boys' pocket or jack-knives, in buffalo,
stag and bone handles, 5c, 10c, 15c.
No. 4. Ladies' pen knives, two blades, in ivory
or bone handles, 15c, 25c.
No. 5. Ladies' pen knives, two and three
blades, pearl handles, in satin-lined cases,
35c, 50c.

Carving Sets.

No. 7. Knife, fork and steel, stag handles, forged steel blades, in satin-lined fancy cases, $1.50, 2.00, 2.50.

No. 8. Knife, fork and steel, stag handles, hand-forged steel blade, in satin-lined leather cases, $3.00, 3.50, 4.00.

No. 9. Knife, fork and steel, stag handles, fancy silver ferrule, hand-forged steel blade, $4.25, 4.50, 5.00, 6.00 ; five-piece sets, $7.50, 8.50.

No. 10. Knife, fork and steel, celluloid handles, hand-forged steel blade, in satin-lined leather cases, $4.00, 4.50.

No. 11. Knife, fork and steel, ivory handle, hand-forged steel blade, in satin-lined leather cases, $6.00, 7.00 ; five-piece sets, $10.00, 12.00.

Silver-Plated Goods.

The celebrated Roger's silver-plated flatware are guaranteed by the maker.

No. 15. Teaspoons, tipped pattern, in satin-lined cases, half-dozen in case, $1.25 ; dessert spoons, $2.05 ; dessert forks, $2.05 ; table forks, $2.50.

No. 16. Teaspoons. shell pattern, in satin-lined cases, half-dozen in case, $1.35 ; dessert spoons, $2.35 ; dessert forks, $2.35; table forks, $2.75.

No. 17. Teaspoons, Flemish or Louis XV. pattern, in satin-lined cases, half-dozen in case, $1.60 ; dessert spoons, $2.50 ; dessert forks, $2.50 ; table forks, $3.00.

No. 18. Sugar spoon. Flemish or Louis XV. pattern, in plush-lined case, 50c ; gold bowls, 75c.

Prices for odd pieces, see Fall and Winter Catalogue, No. 39, page 135.

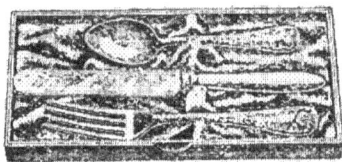

No. 23. Child's set, knife, fork and spoon, in satin-lined case 15c.

No. 24. Child's set, knife, fork and spoon, white metal, silver-plated, in satin-lined case, 25c.

No. 25. Child's set, knife fork and spoon, silver-plated, in plush-lined cases, 50c, 65c, 75c, $1.00.

No. 26. Child's set, knife, fork and spoon, silver-plated, in satin-lined leather case, $1.00, 1.50, 2.00.

No. 27. Child's set, fork and spoon sterling silver ; knife, steel blade, silver plated ; in satin-lined leather cases, $3.00, 3.50, 4.00.

No. 28. Child's napkin rings, silver plated, nicely carved, in satin-lined box, 10c, 15c, 20c, 25c.

Nut Sets.

No. 30. Six picks and one crack, in satin-lined cases, 25c, 35c.

Six picks and one crack, silver plated, in satin-lined cases, 50c, 75c, 85c; in solid oak cases, $1.00, 1.25.

Fruit Sets.

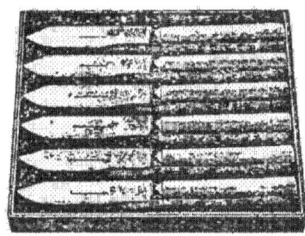

No. 31. Six knives, steel blades and metal handles, silver plated, in satin-lined cases, 85c, $1.00 ; in oak cases, $1.50.

No. 32. Combination fruit and nut sets, silver plated, in satin-lined cases, $2.00 ; in oak cases, $2.50.

Silverware—Quadruple Plate.

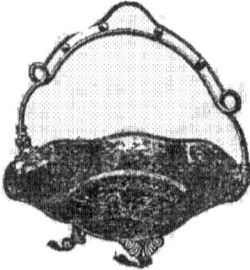

No. 35. Cake basket, satin engraved centre, bright fluted edge, $3.35 ; new designs, gold lined, $4.50, 5.50, 6.00.

No. 36. Nut bowl, handsome design, gold-lined, $5.50; silver-lined, $5.25; other new designs, $6.00, 6.50.

No. 37. Dessert set, satin bright cut, cream pitcher gold-lined, spoon, gold bowl, $4.25.

No. 38.   No. 40.

No. 38. Individual pepper and salt cruet, tinted bottles, $1.65 ; finished in floral designs on frosted bottles, $2.00.

No. 39. Child's cup, silver plated, small, 20c ; medium, 25c ; large size, 40c, 50c.

No. 40. Child's cup, special plate, 50c, 75c, 90c, $1.00.

Child's cup, like cut, $1.50, 1.75, 2.00, 2.50.

For prices and other designs, see Fall and Winter Catalogue, No. 39, Page 134.

No. 41. Bon-bon tray with handle, $1.55; gold-lined, $1.65 ; larger sizes, $2.25, 3.00, 3.50.

No. 42. Fruit bowls, quadruple plate, newest designs, $3.00, 3.50; with tinted bowls, $4.00; 4.50, 5.00; with satin finish and gold, decorations, extra heavy, $5.50, 6.50, 7.25.

No. 43. Bake dishes, satin finish, bright cut, special plate, $4.00, 4.50, 5.00 ; heavy quadruple plate, $6.75, 8.00, 10.00.

Needle Cases.

Assorted needles, in fancy decorated cases, 15c, 20c, 25c, 35c each.

Thimbles.

Silver thimbles, 25c, 50c, 75c.

Silver thimbles, in satin-lined cases, 75c, $1.00.

Silver thimble and embroidery scissors, in satin-lined case, $1.00, $1.25.

Silver thimble and embroidery scissors, in solid leather case, $1.50, 1.75.

Assorted wire hair-pins, in fancy white metal box, 20c.

Fans.

Child's feather fans, feathers on both sides, in cream, pink and blue, 35c, 75c.

Feather fans, feathers on both sides, in cream, pink, blue, nile, mauve, black, 75c.

Finer quality feather fans, newest designs, fancy handles, in above shades, $1.00, 1.50.

Real ostrich feather fans (a new assortment), in white and black, $2.50, 3.00, 3.50, 4.00, 4.50, 5.00, 5.50, 6.00, 6.50, 7.00.

Gauze fans, highly decorated, in white, pink and blue, 50c.

Gauze fans, better quality, newest designs, fancy handles, in black, white, blue and pink, 75c, $1.00, 1.25, 1.50.

Ladies' 6-size Case.

This cut shows a 6-Size Ladies' case. Can be had plain polished, Engine-turned to a shield, or beautifully engraved. It is hunting closed style and pendant set. The movement is a fine 7-jewelled nickel one, of American manufacture, artistically damaskeened, patent safety pinion, and poised balance. An excellent time-keeper.

A16. Above movement, in a solid silver case, $7.

A17. Above movement, in a 5-year gold-filled case, $7.50.

A19. Above movement, in a 14k 20-year gold-filled case, $10.35.

A20. Above movement, in a 10k solid gold case, $18.25.

A21. Above movement, in a 14k solid gold case, $22.50.

A7. We have a very fine American boy's watch, plain, or like cut, with a nickel case, $3.50.

A8. Our special 7-jewelled movement, in a solid silver case, screw back and bezel, 16-size, complete, $5.75.

A9. Our special 7-jewel movement, in 10-k gold-filled 15-year case, $9.50.

A10. The same movement as A9, in 14k gold-filled 20-year case, $12.50.

16-Size Open Face.

NOTE.—If a 15-jewel movement is desired, add $1.25 to the above prices.

For a complete assortment of our 16-size watches, see our Fall and Winter Catalogue, No. 39, page 128.

18-Size Open Face.

The above cut shows the size of cases listed below. The nickel, silver, stiffened, and solid silver cases are plain polished, the others can be had engine-turned or engraved. We pride ourselves in sending the latest designs. The movement is a fine nickel movement, of American manufacture, and known as "The Sun Dial." It has the latest improvements, including a patent safety centre pinion, poised balance, is quick train, has 7 jewels, and is beautifully damaskeened, is also stem-wind and set. This is decidedly the latest production in a reliable watch, and the price will tend to make it a rapid seller, consequently, we advise ordering early.

A1. The above-described movement, in a nickel screw back and Bezel case, $4.00.

A2. The above-described movement, in a silver stiffened case, $6.00.

A3. The above-described movement, in a solid silver 3-oz. screw back and Bezel case, $7.40.

A4. The above-described movement, in a gold-filled 5-year case, $7.20.

A5. The above-described movement, in a 10k gold-filled 15-year case, $8.00.

A6. The above-described movement, in a 14k gold-filled 20-year case, $11.60.

For prices and descriptions of higher grade Waltham and Elgin movements and cases, see our Fall and Winter Catalogue, No. 39.

Work Boxes and Toilet Cases.

Work Boxes.

No. 1.

No. 1. Fancy celluloid work-box, nicely embossed and lined with fittings, 50c.

No. 2. Same box, with satin lining and lithographed top, 75c.

No. 3. Fancy celluloid work-box, embossed and hand-painted top, satin lined and mirror, $1.00.

No. 4. Same as No. 3, with lithographed top, $1.25.

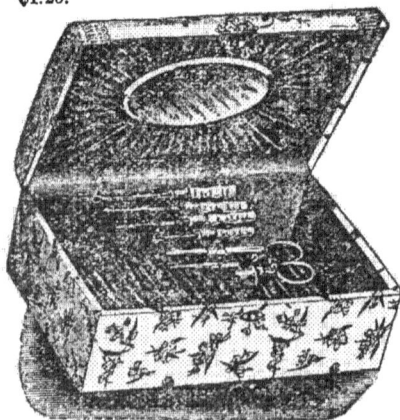

No. 5. Fine celluloid work-box, with plush trimmings, $1.50.

No. 6. Same, with French bevelled mirror, pleated heavy satin and lithographed top, $1.75.

No. 7. Same box, in Dresden china finish, same as cut, $2.00, 2.50.

No. 8. Same, with slanting desk, shaped top, $2.50, 3.00.

Jewel Cases.
(See Cut No. 1.

No. 9. Celluloid jewel case, same shape and style as No. 1, nicely lined, without fittings, 50c.

No. 10. Celluloid jewel case, finely embossed, satin lined, two compartments, $1.00.

No. 11. Celluloid jewel case, hand-painted top, satin lined, separate compartments, movable tray, with lock and key, $1.25.

No. 12. Same case, with lithographed top and extension base, $1.75.

No. 13. Celluloid jewel case, embossed, decorated top, plush trimmings, pleated satin lining, hand-painted, with tray, lock and key, $2.50.

No. 14. Trinket-box, same shape as No. 1 work-box, with three compartments, embossed, celluloid, satin-lined, 50c.

No. 15. Same style, lithographed top, larger size, $1.00.

No. 16. Same style, lithographed top, embossed sides, extension base, four compartments, pleated satin lining, $1.75.

Toilet Cases.

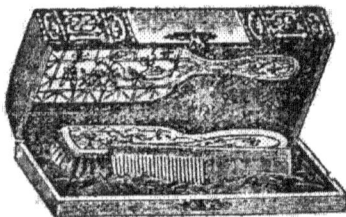

No. 17. Celluloid toilet case, nicely embossed top, satin lined, with brush, comb and bevel plate mirror, $1.00, 1.25 ; smaller size, with plain mirror, 75c.

No. 18. Same set, finished with plush trimmings, $1.25.

No. 19. Celluloid toilet case, same as No. 17, with lithographed and embossed top, $1.75, $2.00 ; lithographed in Dresden patterns, $3.00.

No. 20. Celluloid combination toilet and manicure case, large size brush and mirror, decorated in floral designs, $2.50.

No. 21. Celluloid combination toilet case and manicure set, satin lined, beautiful lithographed top, $3.00, 3.25.

No. 22. Combination toilet and manicure case, floral designs, hand painted, containing brush, comb, bevel mirror, scissor, button hook, nail file and salve box, $3.75 ; with plush trimmings, $4.00.

No. 23. Same set as No. 22, with lithographed top, extension base, $4.50, $5.00 ; same designs, with better fittings and extra large, $6.00, 7.00, 8.00.

Other designs, extra large size, combination toilet and manicure set, complete set of fittings, silk lined and silk corded, beautiful lithographed top, $8.00, 10.00, 12.00.

No. 27. Upright automatic case, raising top, lowering front, full celluloid embossed hand-painted and lithographed decoration, satin lined and silk corded, full combination toilet and manicure set, $8.50, 9.50.

No. 28. Other designs, same style, a little different in shape, $7.00, 8.00.

No. 29. Other designs, with drop front only, $4.50, 5.50, 6.00.

Manicure Sets.

No. 30. Fine celluloid manicure case, embossed

top, extension base, satin lined, complete fittings, $1.25.

No. 31. Same style as No. 30, without extension base, satin lined, $1.00.

No. 32. Same style as No. 30, celluloid case, satin lined, silk corded, lithographed top, $1.50, 1.75.

No. 33. Fine manicure case, same style as No. 30, with best fittings, $2.50, 3.00, 3.50.

Photo Cases.

No. 34. Fine celluloid photo case, with word "Photo" on top, floral decorations, satin lined, $1.00.

No. 35. Same case, with beautiful lithographed top, satin lined, nicely pleated $1.25.

No. 36. Fine celluloid case, nicely embossed and lithographed, double the size of No. 35, in two sections, satin lined, $2.00.

Necktie Boxes.

No. 37. Full celluloid case, nice lithographed top, satin lined, $1.00.

No. 38. Fancy celluloid case, same shape as No. 37, rounded corners, embossed, satin lined, nicely pleated, $1.25, 1.50.

Fan Cases.

No. 39. Same as No. 37, with beautiful decorated top, $1.00.

No. 40. Same style and top as No. 34 photo case, and same case as No. 38, $1.25 and 1.50.

Glove and Handkerchief Boxes.

No. 41. Handkerchief case, celluloid, embossed, lithographed top, satin lined, $1.00.

No. 42. Same case, extension top, $1.75.

No. 43. Glove and handkerchief set, glove box same shape as No. 37, handkerchief box same as No. 41, both nicely lined, 65c each, or $1.25 set.

No. 41.

No. 44. Glove and handkerchief set, same as No. 43, satin lined, 90c each, or $1.75 set.

No. 45. Same set with beautiful lithographed tops, $1.25 each, or $2.25 set.

No. 46. Glove, handkerchief and jewel case combined, fitted with glove stretcher, satin and plush lined, celluloid lithographed top, $2.00.

No. 47. Celluloid glove case, same as No. 37, $1.00.

No. 48. Celluloid glove case, same as No. 38, $1.25, 1.50.

No. 49. Necktie case or glove box, in two sections, fine satin-pleated lining, $2.25.

Cuff and Collar Boxes.

No. 50. Celluloid combination cuff and collar boxes, separate partitions, satin cushions inside, "Cuffs and Collars" nicely lithographed on lid, $1.00.

No. 51. Cuff and collar box, handsomely lithographed, satin lined, nicely pleated, $1.50

No. 52. Same box, lithographed and embossed with gold sprigs, $2.00.

No. 53. Celluloid cuff and collar box, lithographed top, satin lined, with 9-inch extension base, $2.75.

Shaving Cases.

No. 54. Celluloid shaving case, satin lined, fitted with mug and brush, $1.00.

No. 55. Celluloid shaving case, desk shape, nicely embossed, satin lined, extension base, fitted with brush, mug and razor, $1.50.

No. 56. Same set as No. 55, with lithographed top, $2.00.

No. 57. Same set as No. 55, satin lined, plush trimmed, with celebrated K. & B. razor, $3.

No. 58. Celluloid shaving case, extension base, satin lined, lithographed top, finely embossed, fitted with decorated mug, French bevel mirror, brush and razor, $3.00.

No. 59. Celluloid shaving case, embossed sides, fancy lithographed top, extension base, satin lined, with real badger's hair brush, celebrated K. & B. razor $4.50.

No. 60. Same set as No. 59, with celluloid backed hair brush extra, $5.00, 5.50.

Along with our high-class and well made celluloid cases we give a few prices of our cheaper line, made lighter and cheaper; still they will be found serviceable and of pretty designs :

No. 61. Celluloid glove box, satin-lined, hand-painted top, brass feet, 85c.

No. 62. Celluloid glove box, painted top, brass feet, 50c.

No. 63. Celluloid handkerchief box, nicely lined, painted top, brass feet, 50c.

No. 64. Celluloid handkerchief box, satin-lined, hand-painted top, pretty designs, 75c, $1.00.

No. 65. Celluloid photo box, brass feet, newest designs, 75c, $1.00.

No. 66. Children's handkerchief and glove sets, with celluloid trimming, with "Gloves and Handkerchiefs" nicely painted on top, set of two pieces, 25c.

No. 67. Child's celluloid work-box, including fittings, 25c.

No. 68. Child's celluloid work-box, basket shape, including fittings, 25c.

No. 69. Celluloid jewel-boxes, brass feet, square or heart-shape, 25c.

No. 70. Celluloid calendars, hand-painted floral designs, with days, weeks and month printed on satin ribbon, for hanging on the wall, 15c.

No. 71. Celluloid calendars, owl-shape, with parasol, 25c.

No. 72. Celluloid holder, pretty design, 25c.

Travelling Cases.

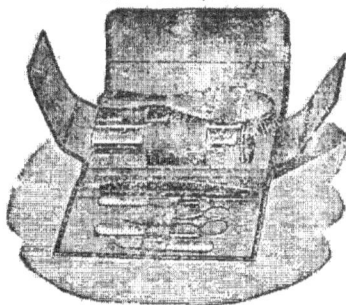

No. 24. Gents' leather travelling companions, containing brush, comb, tooth-brush and soap box, $1.00, 1.50, 2.00.

No. 25. Gents' travelling companions, solid leather, full fittings, $3.50, 4.25, 6.00, 8.00.

No. 26. Ladies' travelling companions, full fittings, $4.00, 5.00, 6.50, 8.50.

No. 27. Gents' travelling bags, including fittings, $12.00, 15.00, 18.00, 25.00.

Purses.

No. 78. Ladies' combination purse and card case, in genuine seal leather, with fancy ticket pockets, inside steel frame, 60c.

No. 79. Same style purse, in genuine calf leather or crushed morocco, 75c.

No. 80. Ladies' combination purse and card case, in seal grain leather, description of No. 78, with white metal corners, 35c, 50c.

COMBINATION PURSE—OPEN.

No. 81. Ladies' combination purse and card case, crushed morocco, leather lined, with one large ticket pocket, etc., with sterling silver corners, $1.00.

CLOSED.

No. 82. Same purse as No. 81, in genuine seal, black only, with sterling silver corners, $1.00, 1.25, 1.50.

No. 83. Ladies' combination purse and card case, description of No. 81, calf lined, in crushed morocco or genuine seal leather, with large beaded sterling silver corners, $1.75, 2.00.

No. 84. Ladies' combination purse and card case, in polished alligator, crushed morocco or seal leather, polished calf, leather lined, with five pockets and ticket pocket, $2.75, 3.00.

No. 85. Same purse as No. 78, with heavy sterling silver corners, $4.00.

No. 86. Ladies' purse, in lizard or crushed morocco leather, five pockets and card case, leather and silk lined, clasp on outside, beautiful finish, $2.50.

No. 87. Same purse as No. 81, in alligator or seal leather, nicely polished, 3.00.

No. 88. Ladies' long pocket book, size 5½ x 2½ inches, in lizard and crushed morocco leather, with five pockets, one gold pocket, two ticket pockets and one card pocket, with strap and clasp on the outside, best polished finish, $3.50.

No. 90. Ladies' bag-shaped purse, in alligator and lizard leather, polished, chamois lined, four pockets, riveted frame, $1.75.

No. 91. Same purse as No. 12, in seal leather, $1.25.

Gents' Bill Books.

No. 115. Gents' bill book, in seal grain leather, leather lined, safety bill pocket, size when closed, 3½ in. by 7½ in., 65c, 75c.

No. 116. Gents' bill book, in real seal leather, calf lined, with card and ticket pocket, $2.25, 2.50.

Gents' Letter Books.

No. 117. Gents' letter book, in seal grain leather, four pockets, size 4 in. by 6½ in., 60c;

No. 118. Same, in seal leather, calf lined, 3½ in. by 6 in., $1.00.

No. 119. Gents' letter book, genuine seal or alligator leather, calf lined, ticket and stamp pockets, polished finish, 4 in. by 6½ in., seal $1.75; alligator, $2.50.

No. 120. Gents' strap pocket-book, with 5 pockets and secret bill-book, 75c, $1.00, 1.50

Card Cases.

No. 121. Gents' card cases, genuine seal leather, with ticket pocket, size 2½ x 4 in., 75c.

No. 122. Gents' card case, alligator leather, silk lined, polished finish, $1.00.

No. 123. Ladies' card case, in seal grain leather, black only, 35c.

No. 124. Ladies' card case, real seal leather, seal lined, with ticket pockets, nicely finished, $1.00.

Ladies' Hand Bags.

No. 125. Ladies' hand bag, in morocco leather, leather lined, leather handles, steel frames, size 5 x 8 in., $2.00, 2.50.

No. 126. Same as No. 125, with card and ticket pocket on outside, 5 x 6½ in., $2.00, 2.75; better qualities, in polished leathers, best lining, $3.00, 4.50, 6.00, 8.00.

No. 127. Boston-shaped bags, morocco leather, silk lined, leather rope handles, spring catch, 10 in. long, 4 in. deep, $2.50, 2.75, 3.00.

No. 128. Music holders, satin lined, leather handles, spring catch on side, size when closed, 6 x 15 in., in seal grain leather, $1.50; alligator grain, $2.25; genuine alligator, highly polished, $3.00.

Umbrellas.

No. 105. Ladies' black umbrella, with best silk and wool cover, size 23-inch, steel rods, paragon frames, large variety Dresden, horn and natural wood handles, with silver mountings, $2.00, 2.50, 3.00.

No. 106. Ladies' black umbrellas, 23-inch, taffeta, silk and satin de chene covers, best paragon frames and steel rods, latest designs in handles, pearl, Dresden and horn, with gold and sterling silver, mountings, $3.00, 3.50, 4.00.

No. 107. Ladies' black umbrellas, pure silk covers, fancy handles, pearl and horn, with sterling silver and gold mountings, steel rods and light paragon frames, to roll very small, $5.00, 5.50, 6.00, 7.00.

No. 108. Gents' black umbrellas, 25-inch, best satin de chene covers, steel rods and good strong paragon frames, natural wood handles, knobs or crooks, with sterling silver mountings, $2.50, 3.00, 3.50.

No. 109. Gents' steel or wood rod umbrellas, pure silk covers, paragon frames, cherry or Congo handle, straight or crook, with gold and sterling silver mountings, $4.00, 5.00, 6.00.

No. 110. Gents' 25-inch umbrellas, taffeta silk, in leather cases, steel rods and paragon frames, $3.50, 4.00.

No. 111. Ladies' shot silk umbrellas, in all colors, steel rods and paragon frames, handle to match silk, $3.50, 4.00.

Walking Sticks and Canes

No. 112. Burnt Congo sticks, the best quality, sterling silver mountings, medium, large or small size sticks, 75c, $1.00, 1.50.

No. 113. Heavier mountings, $2.00, 2.75.

No. 114. Gold mountings, $1.00, 1.50.

Drugs, Perfumery, Brushes, Soaps.

Gold Label Perfume.

Our Gold Label Perfume is a quadruple essence of flowers and floral bouquets, and is put up in many different styles as follows:

No. 838. Decorated handled cut stoppered vase, holding about 3½ ozs, in fancy box, $1.00 ea.
No. 830. Fancy decorated jug, cut stopper, holding about 1¾ ozs, in fancy box, 60c each.
No. 2165. Cut glass bottle and stopper, 8-sided, ½ oz bottle, in fancy box, 35c each.

No. 1342. Cut glass stopper, flat-pressed bottle, 1 oz, in fancy box, 50c each.
No. 2636. Cut glass stopper, flat-pressed bottle, 1¼ oz, 50c each.
No. 1306. Cut glass stopper, flat-pressed bottle, 1¼ oz, 50c each.

No. 2175. Cut glass bottle and stopper, 8-sided, 1 oz bottle, in fancy box, 50c each.

No. 2185. Cut glass 8-sided oval, about 1¼ oz bottle, in fancy box, 75c each.
No. 426. Cut glass 4-sided flat, about 1 oz bottle, in fancy box, 75c each.

No. 2013. Cut glass 10-sided round, 1¼ oz, squat shape, 75c each.
No. 2182. Cut glass bottle and stopper, 10-sided bottle, cone shaped, 1¼ oz, 75c each.
No. 2094. Fancy cut glass bottle and stopper, in fancy box, 1¼ oz, 75c each.

No. 2166. Plain cut glass bottle and stopper, 3-sided, in fancy box, ¾ oz, 75c.

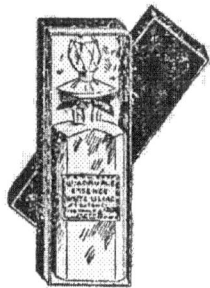

No. 2160. Plain cut glass bottle and stopper, 4-sided flat, tall, holds about 2 ozs, in fancy box, $1.00 each.

No. 2039. Fancy cut glass bottle and stopper, square squat shape, 6-oz bottle, in fancy box, $3.00 each.
No. 2085 Flat 6-sided cut glass bottle, 3¼ ozs, in fancy box, $1.75 each.
No. 2130. Cut glass 10-sided bottle, holds 4 ozs, in fancy box, $1.75 each.

No. 190. Plain round bottle, with metal sprinkler top, in fancy box, 40c each ; in bulk, Gold Label perfume is 35c oz, except Reviera Violet, which is 60c oz, and is put up in a cut stoppered pressed bottle, in a fancy box, 75c each.

The following list of odors we have in Gold Label perfume, at 35c oz.

Myrtle Blossom.	Lign Aloe.
Parma Violet.	Heliotrope.
Canada Bouquet.	Jasmin.
White Lilac.	Tube Rose.
Wood Violet.	Royal Pink.
Mona Bouquet.	Patchouli.
Royal Bouquet.	Wallflowers.
Military Bouquet.	Jonquille.
Ontario Bouquet.	Opopanax.
Florida Zephyrs.	Violet.
Golden Moments.	Magnolia.
Japan Amarylis.	Crab Apple.
Jockey Club.	White Rose.
Lily of the Valley.	Musk.
Stephanotis.	Mignonette.
Parisian Bouquet.	Tea Rose.
Golden Bell.	Moss Rose.
Honeysuckle.	Sweet Briar.
White Heliotrope.	Rondeletia.
Ylang Ylang.	Millefleur.
Hawthorn Blossom.	Mareschale.
Ess. Bouquet.	

Blue Label Perfume.

In Bulk, 20c oz, and in round bottles, with sprinkler top, in a fancy box, price, 25c. It can be put in fancy cut glass bottles, price of bottle to be added to price of perfume. (See list of fancy bottles below.) The fol-

lowing is a list of the odors, which are all true to name :

White Rose.	Violet.
Lily of the Valley.	Ylang Ylang.
Frangipanni.	Wood Violet.
New Mown Hay.	White Lilac.
Patchouli.	Mignonette.
Crab Apple.	Heliotrope.
Jockey Club.	Stephanotis.

Reviera Violet—The most fragrant and lasting, while at the same time delicate odor of sweet violets that is manufactured, price, 60c oz.

Little Folk's Perfumes.

We put four bottles of choice perfumery, any assortment of the following six odors. It makes an elegant and popular little present for children, as its name implies.

Jockey Club. White Lilac.
White Rose. Wood Violet.
Heliotrope. Lily of the Valley.
Price, 25c box.

Fancy Cut Glass Bottles. Empty.

No. 21524. Elegantly cut, tapered from base to top, capacity 1¾ ozs, stands almost 7 inches high, price 75c.

No. 186937. Fancy cut bottle, round squat, holds 2 ozs, 25c.

No. 186937A. Fancy cut bottle. 6-sided, pyramid, holds 1 oz, 25c.

No. 21460. Fancy cut bottle, squat base, long tapered neck, holds 1¼ ozs, 25c.

No. 19900. Fancy cut bottle, three-sided, holds 1¼ ozs, 25c.

No. 2039. Plain cut, square squat bottle, corners cut. 6 ozs, 75c.

No. 2085. Plain flat 8-sided bottle, holds 3¼ ozs, 40c.

No. 2130. Plain round 10-sided bottle, holds 4 ozs, 35c.

No. 2160.—Flat cut glass bottle, corners cut off, holds 2 ozs, 30c.

No. 2185. Oval cut glass bottle, holds 1⅛ ozs, 25c.

No. 2094. Round cut glass bottle, tapers to topand bottom, holds 1¼ ozs, 25c.

No. 2166. Three sides, plain cut bottle, holds ¾ ozs, 25c.

No. 426. Nearly sqaure plain cut bottle, holds 1 oz, 25c.

No. 2013. Squat 10-sided round plain cut, bevelled top and bottom, holds 1¼ ozs, 25c.

No. 2182. Ten-sided, round plain cut, tapered from base to neck, holds 1⅛ ozs, 25c.

No. 2175. Eight-sided round, sides only cut, bottle holds 1 oz, cut stopper, 15c.

No. 2165. Eight-sided round, sides only cut. bottle holds ½ oz, cut stopper, 10c.

No. 2004. Cut stopper, pressed flat bottle, holds 3 ozs, 20c.

No. 1342. Cut stopper, pressed flat bottle, holds 1 oz, 10c.
No. 2636. Cut stopper, pressed oval bottle, holds 1¼ ozs, 10c.
No. 830. Cut stopper, Bohemian-handled jug, fancy decoration, holds 1¼ ozs, 25c.

No. 838. Cut stopper, Bohemian vase, two handles, fancy decoration, 3½ ozs, 30c.
Decorated Bohemian bisque handled vase, cork stopper, holds 4 ozs., 15c; holding 1½ ozs., 10c.

When we have sold out of any special style of bottle we will not be able to repeat, but will have to substitute the nearest that we have.

Atkinson's Perfumes.

1 oz. Bottles, 50c; 2 oz Bottles, 85c.

Following is our list of odors at 50c, and those marked with an asterisk we have at 85c as well as 50c:

*White Rose. *Wood Violet.
Wild Roses. Wild Violets.
Ylang Ylang. White Moss Rose.
White Lily. Wild Flowers.
Wild Hyacinth.
    *White Lilac.
Wall Flowers.
    White Heliotrope.
Violet. *Stephanotis.
Seringa. Sweet Briar.
Sweet Pea. Opoponax.
Peau d'Espagne.
    New Mown Hay.

Musk. Myrtle Flowers.
Mignonette. Lign Aloe.
*Lily of the Valley.
Jockey Club. *Lilac.
Hall's Wood Violet, 45c, 75c.
Hall's Heliotrope, 45c, 75c.
Crown perfumery, Crab-apple, 60c, $1.25.
Crown perfumery, Peau d'Espagne, $1.25.
Crown perfumery, Violet De Parme, 60c.
Colgate's Cashmere Bouquet, 60c, $1.00 bottle.
Colgate's perfumes, different odors, 60c, $1.00.
Lundburgh's Swiss Lilac, 60c, $1.00.

Toilet Waters and Sundries.

Our toilet waters are a superior product and are true to odor. For Christmas presents a bottle would be acceptable to anyone, as it can also be used as a perfume, in 8 oz. bottles, 75c; 4 oz. bottles, 40c.

The following is a list of odors—

Violet. Lily of the Valley.
Heliotrope. Rose.
    White Lilac.

Colgate's cashmere bouquet toilet water, 8 oz, $1.00; 3 oz, 50c; 1 oz, 20c.
Colgate's Violet Toilet Water, 8 oz, $1.00; 3 oz, 50c; 1 oz, 20c.
Murray & Lanman's Florida water, 40c.
Wakulla Florida water, 35c.
Wakulla Lavender water, 4 oz bottle, 25c.
Eau de Cologne, long green "Eaton's," 25c.
Eau de Cologne, 4 oz, bottle, 25c; 8 oz, 50c.
Eau de Cologne, genuine small, 30c; regular, 60c.
Aromatic toilet vinegar, 4 oz bottle, 25c.

Lewis' Lavender salts, in green bottles, 20c and 35c.
Lewis' flora' salts, in green bottles, 20c and 35c.
Fancy cut glass bottles of smelling salts, 25c, 35c, 50c, 75c, $1.00, 1.25, 1.50, 1.75, 2.00, 2.50, 3.00.
Crown Lavender salts, 35c and 60c bottle.
Aromatic vinegar (for headache is refreshing, etc.), in cut glass bottles, 25c up.

Sachet Powders.

Sachet powder, 10c bottle; by mail, in envelope, postpaid, 20c per oz. ¼ oz. is the smallest quantity we pay postage on. We have the following odors

Jockey Club.
Stephanotis.
White
    Heliotrope.
Wood Violet. White Rose.
    Cashmere Bouquet.
Violet. White Lilac.
Lily of the Valley.

Face Powders.

Bloom of Canada, a very highly perfumed semi-transparent powder, does not dry the skin, in flesh, cream or white, 25c

Moss Rose, pink, white or cream, 10c box.

All others as Catalogue No. 39.

Perfume Sprays or Atomizers.

Fancy perfume atomizers in many different styles, colors, shapes and prices, from 25c to $3.50. It is better to tell color and price, as it would be an endless undertaking to describe all the styles.

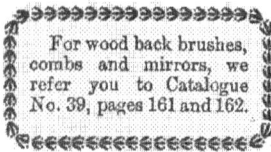

For wood back brushes, combs and mirrors, we refer you to Catalogue No. 39, pages 161 and 162.

Thermometers.

7-in. Japanned tin thermometer, 10c each.

8-in. Japanned tin thermometer, 12½c each.

10-in. japanned tin thermometer, 15c each.

12-in. japanned tin thermometer, 20c each.

Glass dairy thermometer, 10c each.

Wood-backed thermometer, 15c.

7-in. cabinet wood-backed thermometer, 25c.

8-in. cabinet wood-backed thermometer, 30c.

10-in. cabinet wood-backed thermometer, 35c.

8-in. magnifying lens, wood back, 50c.

10-in. magnifying lens, wood back, 75c.

16-in. cabinet wood thermometer, 75c.

Fancy thermometers, 75c, $1.00, 1.25, 1.50, 2.00, 2.50.

Small button thermometer, with pin to stick in coat, a novelty, 25c.

Barometer and thermometer, cottage, 20c.

Barometer and thermometer, tin panel, 15c.

Barometer and thermometer, polished oak frame, 60c.

Maximum registering thermometer, $1.00.

Minimum registering thermometer, $1.00.

Maximum and minimum combined, $2.50.

Art thermometers for fancy work, 2-inch, 5c ; 2½-inch, 7c; 3-inch, 8c ; 3½ or 4-inch, 10c ; 4½ or 5-inch, 13c.

Bronze Powder

For renewing gilt picture frames, gilding ornaments or any kind of fancy work. A good gilding liquid may be made as follows : To one teaspoonful of good copal varnish add six teaspoonsful of turpentine, then mix a little of the liquid and bronze powder at a time.

Finest unoxidizable bronze, per oz, 25c.

Fine unoxidizable bronze, per oz, 20c.

Good unoxidizable bronze, per oz, 15c.

Unoxidizable bronze, a very fair quality, 10c ounce.

Coloured bronze, all shades, green, blue, red, etc., 20c oz.

Soaps.

For toilet soaps we refer you to page 162 and 163 of No. 39 Catalogue, all of which we can supply except Fancy Fruit Soaps, which we may not be able to furnish for Christmas trade.

The T. Eaton Co., Limited, cream of almonds toilet soap, 6 cakes, 25c.

The T. Eaton Co., Limited, cream of elderflower and cucumber, 6 cakes, 25c.

The T. Eaton, Co., Limited, cream of oatmeal, 5 cakes, 25c.

The T. Eaton Co., Limited, Cream of Roses, 6 cakes, 25c.

Candles.

Christmas tree candles, toy, 18 to box, 24 to box, 36 to box, 48 to box, price per box, 10c; 18 small candles in box, 5c.

Colored paraffin candles, 15c and 30c.

Colored candles, twist or rope pattern, 35c lb.

Paraffin candles, 6 or 12 to lb., 12½c lb.

Brownie lanterns, complete, for Christmas trees, etc., 50c doz.

Night lights; 60c doz.

Fairy night lights, 25c box.

Clark's fancy night lights, 60c doz.

Candy Department.

FOR Christmas trees, Santa Claus stockings, etc., our Christmas mixed creams are the best value that can be obtained, being good wholesome candy, and nicely made.

For Christmas trees, etc., by the pail of 35 lbs., $3.50, pail included ; by the pound, 10c lb.
We have cheaper mixed candy, 6c, 8c lb.
Chocolates, 12½c lb.
Cream dates, 15c lb.
Cream almonds, 20c lb.
Callard & Bowser's butterscotch, 10c, 20c pkge.
French fruit, crystallized, assorted, 60c lb.
Maple butterscotch, 20c lb.
Maple cream, best, 20c lb.
Maple cream, good, 10c lb.
Cocoanut cream, pink and white, 15c lb.
Cocoanut rock taffy, 15c lb.
Almond rock taffy, 15c lb.
Walnut rock taffy, 15c lb.
Walnut bar, 20c lb.
Everton rock, 15c lb.
Peanut rock, 15c lb.
Almond tablets. 15c lb.
Butter wafers 15c lb
Maple walnut pudding, 25c lb.
Marrow Bone, best, 20c lb.
Marrow Bone, good, 12½c lb.
Crystallized ginger, 25c lb.
The following chocolates may be had at 30c lb.: Pineapple, ginger, walnut, almond, lemon, orange, coffee, crisps, nougat, raspberry, strawberry, black currant, vanilla, cocoanut.
Marsh mallow drops, finest, 30c lb.
Chocolate dipped caramels, best, 25c lb.
Chocolate dipped caramels, good, 12½c lb.
Jelly fig bon bons, 15c lb.
Jelly date bon bons, 15c lb
Cream dates, 15c lb.
Cream figs, 12½c lb.
Cream candies, special Christmas mixture, many flavors and shapes, extra value, 10c lb., in 1 lb. or 5 lb. boxes.
Buttercups, best quality, nut centres, 20c lb.
Buttercups, good quality, nut centres, 12c lb.
Pearls, a highly flavored compressed lozenge, assorted, or any of the following flavors : Lemon, rose, musk, wintergreen, XXX mint, cayenne, violet, chocolate, Ylang ylang, heliotrope, cinnamon, white rose, clove, ginger, 30c lb.

Cream almonds, 20c lb.
Cream burnt almonds, 20c lb.
Peppermint shrimps, 20c lb.
Peppermint lozenges, 15c lb.
Peppermint lozenges, Gibson's XXX English, 50c lb.
Peppermint lozenges, Gibson's curiously strong, 80c lb.
Conversation lozenges, assorted colors, finest quality, good mottoes, 20c lb.
Solazzie licorice, 60c lb.
Licorice pellets, 60c lb.
Licorice, sugar coated, 20c lb.
Tom Thumb mixed sweets, 20c lb.
Gibson's fruit tablets and drops, 25c lb.
    " cough drops, 25c lb.
    " lime fruit tablets, 25c lb.
    " horehound drops, 25c lb.
    " bath pipe lozenges or stick, 50c lb.
    " black currant lozenges, 80c lb.
    " chlorodyne lozenges, 80c lb.
    " cayenne lozenges, 45c lb.
    " charcoal lozenges, 70c lb.
    " musk lozenges, 70c lb.
    " Multum in parvo musk lozenges, $1.00.
    " curiously strong ginger lozenges, 80c lb.
    " delectable jujubes, 70c lb.
    " voice jujubes, 70c lb.
    " glycerine pastilles, 70c lb.

Fancy Boxes of Candy.

Elegant fancy box, holds about a pound of finest assorted chocolates, or bon bons, or assorted, as desired, 50c box.
Fancy box of candies, as above, 40c lb.
Fine chocolates, assorted, 30c lb.
Chocolate burnt almonds, 40c lb.
Good chocolates, 16 flavors, 20c lb.
Good bon bons, assorted, 20c lb.
Assorted boxes of candies, in fancy boxes—1 lb boxes, 15c, 20, 25c, 30c ; ½ lb boxes, 10c, 15c, 20c box.

Cossaques, Crackers, or Bon Bons.

No. 1070. A cheap and effective box of somebody's luggage, in white, colored and gold papers ; packed 1 doz crackers in box, 15c.
No. 1071. An extra large and attractive box of somebody's luggage, one doz in box, 20c.

No. 760. A box of one doz crackers, ornamented with flags and Father Xmas, and contains an assortment of surprises and mottoes, specially adapted for children, 20c.
No. 800. **Latest**—Made in an assortment of fancy colored papers, embellished in gold and ornamented with French clowns, containing hats, masks, toys, etc., 20c.

No. 700. **Jewel**—Made in gold and rainbow colors, ornamented with heads of eastern children, and containing the latest novelties in miniature jewels. Each box bears a characteristic label illustrating the contents, 25c.

No. 801. The crackers are in pale pink, dark blue and gold, ornamented with pictures of crying and laughing babies, containing all the latest puzzles, with new and amusing puzzle mottoes, 20c.

No. 732. Made in assorted colors, with brilliant gelatine centres, ornamented with artistic pictures of skating children, and containing a variety of grotesque hats, caps and bonnets, 25c.
No. 763. Made in attractive gold, crimson and blue papers, ornamented in the centre with pantomime characters, and containing a variety of new and amusing puzzles, 30c.
No. 805. Containing dog-masks, grotesque head dresses and other novelties with amusing love mottoes. The box is labelled with an attractive picture representing a family of puppy dogs destroying crackers, 35c.
No. 764. **Hat Box**—The design of the crackers is in gold and assorted tinted papers, ornamented with little children emerging from various kinds of hat boxes, while the contents comprise all the latest novelties in grotesque hats, caps and bonnets, with new and original love mottoes, 35c.
No. 806. **Native Japanese Crackers**—Of marvellous value ; made in real Japanese papers of assorted designs, containing all the latest novelties in Japanese toys, masks, heads, caps, etc., imported direct from Japan. The crackers are packed in elegantly decorated boxes of native design, 35c.

No. 766. This box is mounted with an attractive label representing an interior scene of an Eastern palace, while the crackers are printed in gold and various colors, decorated in the centre with Oriental children, and contain rings, pins, charms, brooches, pendants, etc., 35c.

No. 767. **Granny's Gift Box**—Containing all the latest novelties in miniature toys for boys and girls. The crackers are made in a choice blending of heliotrope, orange and yellow, decorated with children in fancy costume. The box is mounted with an exquisite picture of Granny presenting crackers to the little ones, 50c.

No. 808: **Grandpapa's Xmas Box**— Containing grandpapa's head, collar and moustache, etc., with various toy and jewel novelties. The crackers are made in pale pink and dark green with gelatine centres,

ornamented with old-fashioned children, and forms a delightful companion box to Granny's Gift Box, 50c.

No. 510. **Musical Toy Crackers**—The greatest novelty for juveniles ever produced. In twelve crackers are found twelve different musical toys, such as bagpipes, trumpets, Jews' harps, mouth harmonicans, mirlitons, and many other musical novelties. Made in gelatine, with printed ends representing music, and ornamented with pictures of children. The box has a specially attractive label illustrating the contents, 75c.

No. 772. The crackers are made in brilliant shades of various colored gelatine, the ends of which represent garlands of holly and mistletoe frosted, and producing a glistening effect. The centres are ornamented with Father Christmas figures, while the crackers contain all the latest novelties, and are packed in decorated boxes surmounted with a label representing Father Christmas travelling from the Arctic regions, $1.00.

No. 777. The most brilliant crackers ever produced, the centres being made of fire-red gelatine, and the ends of fire bronze; ornamented with characters representing the various members of the London and Provincial fire brigades, while the crackers contain firemen's hats and helmets, together with specially prepared colored fires, producing a marvellous effect in a darkened room. The box is mounted with an attractive label, illustrating an exciting scene at a London fire, $1.00.

Drug Department.

We have the most complete stock of Drugs and Drug Sundries in Canada, and at the very lowest prices for first quality drugs. Our dispensing is all done by qualified druggists, and is checked before leaving department. We refer you to Catalogue No. 37, page 123 to page 137, and Catalogue No. 39, page 151 to page 163.

Toys and Games.

THE following lines are by no means a complete list of our toys and games, but merely a few holiday hints which, we trust, will be suggestive of just such articles as the little folks especially, enjoy on Christmas morning. *We do not exchange Dolls, Toys or Games.*

Dolls and Doll Articles.

Nankeen body, china head and limbs, painted, 5c, 10c, 15c each.
Kid body dolls, 10c to $6.00 each.
Jointed dolls, 10c to $15.00 each.
Hair stuffed dolls, 10c, 15c, 20c, 25c each.
Nigger dolls, jointed, 25c to 75c each.
Dressed dolls, 15c to $5.00 each.
Dolls' heads, 10c to 20c.

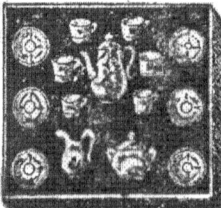

Dolls' shoes, 5c to 20c pair.
Dolls' fans, 10c each.
Dolls' stockings, 5c, 10c pair.
Dolls' wigs, 25c to $1.00 each.
Dolls' cabs, without top, 75c, $1.00; with top, $1.25, 1.50, 1.75.
Dolls' dishes, each set put up in a neat box, from 10c to $2.50 per set.

Miscellaneous Toys.

Tin cart and horse, 25c to $1.00 each.
Pencil set, consisting of wood box and penholder, pencil and knife, 15c to 50c each.
Magic lanterns, 50c to $2.50 each.
Steamboats with engines, $1.25 to 4.00 each.
Steam engines, 75c to $6.00 each.

Toy whips, 5c to 25c each.
Toy baby carriages, tin, 10c to 25c each.
Mechanical toys, 25c to 75c each.
Rattles, 5c to 25c each.
Blocks and cubes, 10c to $1.25 set.
Mechanical bicycle riders, 25c, 50c each.
Musical tops, 10c to 50c each.
Child's enamelled cooking utensils, 10c to 50c set.
Swords, 10c to 50c each.
Paint boxes, 10c to 75c each.
Drawing slates, 10c to 35c each.
Pile-up blocks, 10c to 75c set.
Fur animals, dogs, sheep, etc., 15c to $1.50 each.
Wood horses, 10c to 75c.
Wood horse and cart, 25c to 75c each.
Skin horses and cart, $1.00 to 2.50.
Santa Claus, 5c, 10c, 25c.
Noah's arks, 10c to 25c.
Surprise boxes (Jack-in-the-box), 8c, 10c.

Trumpets and tops, 5c to 50c each.

Toy carts, wood wheels and painted body, 15c each.

Tin trains, 15c to $1.00 each.
Tin engines, 10c to 50c each.
Hot air engines, $1.25 to 6.00 each.

Boys' velocipedes, $1.65 to 3.00.
Girls' tricycles, plush seat and back, $3.75 to 8.00.

Shoofly rockers, large size, extra strong, 60c, 75c each.
Waggons, hardwood bodies and bent rail, $1.25, 1.75 each.
Buckboards, 1 seat, $2.00 ; 2 seats, 2.25.
Skates, 50c to $2.75 pair.

Sleighs, 35c to $1.25 each.

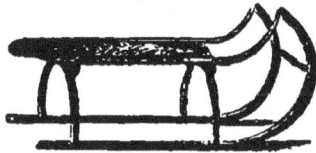

Toy wheelbarrow, wood painted red, 15c each.

Sleds, 15c, 20c, 25c each.

Toy wheelbarrows, metal body and turned steel wheels, 65c, 75c, 90c each.

We do not exchange

DOLLS
TOYS
or GAMES.

Games.

15-cent Board Games—Go Bang, Luck, Red Riding Hood, Steeple Chase, and News Boy.
Other Board Games at 25c to $1.25 each—Business, Penny Post, Prisoner of Zenda, Golf and Limited Mail.

Crokinole boards, complete with discs, 60c and 90c.

Carom boards, complete with marbles, $1.15 ea.

Fort, complete with marbles and cue, 70c.

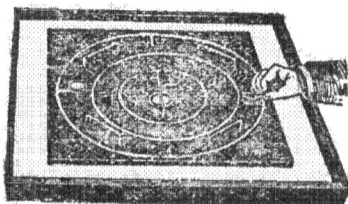

Improved crokinole, 85c.

10-cent—Peter Coddles, Authors, Snap, Cinderella, Old Maid and Robinson Crusoe.
Pillow Dex, the newest and funniest game out, 25c and 50c each complete; rubber bladders for Pillow Dex, to replace those which burst, 5c each.
Christmas tree decorations, tinsel, 2 pkgs for 5c.
Christmas tree ornaments, 25c doz, 50c doz and 70c doz.
Lanterns for Christmas trees, colored glass sides, 5c and 10c each.
Dominoes, 10c, 15c, 25c and 50c per set.
Checker boards, 10c to 75c each.
Checkers, 10c to 50c per set.
Chess men, 60c and 75c per set.

Fireside Educational Games.

The newest card games, each of which is not only very interesting, but highly instructive, enamelled and highly finished, put up in brilliant colored boxes.

Strange People—Depicting different dress, manners and customs of the nations of the world.

Maple Grove—Introducing all kinds of maple leaves, printed in colors.

Population—Showing maps and population of all principal countries in the world.

Flags—Showing national flags of all the principal countries of the world.

In Castle Land—Illustrating the principal castles of the old world.

Nationalities—Showing the different nationalities of the world.

Artists—Showing the world's most popular and famous paintings.

Your choice of any of these games for 25c.

For fancy china, bric-a-brac, vases, china tea sets, cut glass, musical goods, lamps, etc., see our Fall and Winter Catalogue, No. 39, from page 175 to page 190.

Musical Goods.

We do not exchange Musical Goods.

Guitars.

No. 9. Ideal, maple imitation mahogany, machine head, German silver raised frets, position dots, rosewood fingerboard, good quality, $4.00.

No. 10. Maple imitation rosewood, imitation mahogany neck, highly polished rosewood fingerboard and bridge, pearl position dots, German silver frets, inlaid sound hole, $6.00.

No. 1. Imperial antique oak, highly polished mahogany neck, rosewood fingerboard and bridge, pearl position dots, inlaid sound hole, $9.00.

No. 1½. Similar to No. 1, but in concert size, $10.00.

No. 2, Imperial guitar, rosewood, highly polished, similar to No. 1, standard size, $12.00; concert $15.00.

Mandolins.

No. 88. The "Alabama," mahogany and maple ribbed shell, yellow front, special, $5.00.

No. 89. The "Arizona," mahogany and maple 7-ribbed shell, white front and shell guard plate, a beauty, $7.50.

No. 103. The "Hudson," bird's-eye maple (rosewood finish) and maple 7-ribbed shell, $9.00.

No. 108. "Rochester," rosewood and bird's-eye maple 9-ribbed shell, $12.50.

A collection of high class mandolins, which, in tone and appearance, cannot be surpassed, $15.00, 16.50.

Violins.

These prices do not include Bows.

No. 18. Red or brown shaded, $1.00.

No. 1261. Dark brown, highly polished, better quality, $2.00.

No. 33. Conservatory model, red shaded, highly polished, $3.00.

No. 100E. Straduarius, dark brown shaded, fine ebony trimmings, $4.00

No. 178. Stainer, red shaded, extra good value, highly polished, $5.00.

No. 886. Paganini concert violin, amber shaded, highly polished, fine tone and finish, $7.

No. 893. Wieniawski violin, d'artist, dark shaded, elegantly finished and fine tone, $12.

No. 313. Conservatory Straduari, brown and amber shaded, highly polished, fine trimming, well made and good tone, a splendid instrument in every respect, $10.00.

Any of the above, over $4.00 in price, can be furnished in ⅞ size, at the same price.

Accordions.

No. 1196¾. Ideal, miniature size, ebonized frames, open action nickel keys, two stops, two sets of reeds, $2.00.

No. 195½. Ideal, ebonized mouldings, double bellows, nickel

corners and clasps, German silver reeds, open nickel keys, fancy gilt borders, $2.50.

No. 173. "Imperial," small size, 10 keys, 2 stops, 3 bass keys, $3.50.

No. 480. Light colored, concert size, extra fine tone, $9.00.

Autoharps.

No. 10. 3 bars, producing 3 chords, $1.95.

No. 20. 4 bars, producing 4 chords, $2.15.

No. 25. 5 bars, producing 5 chords, $2.50.

No. 30. 6 bars, producing 6 chords, concert size, $4.00.

No. 35. 10 stops, producing 10 chords, new covered bar system, a most beautiful instrument, $5.00.

Mouth Organs.

No. 1601. The Champion, silver reeds, nickel finish, all keys, 10c each.

No. 951. The Silver Medal, bone mouth piece, nickel finish, 15c each.

No. 9811. Navy harp, unexcelled quality, heavy nickel plated sides, 20c each.

"The Star," silver reeds, full sized case, double reeded, 20c each.

Marine Band, one of the newest and best, heavy nickel plated sides, 25c each.

No. 711. "David's Harp," celluloid cover, double reeds, 35c each.

No. 3401. "David's Harp," celluloid cover, large size 50c each.

The "Up-to-Date," concert size, in handsome black case, satin lined, 50c each.

Imperial harp, double reeded, sweet tone, concert size, 75c each.

Bibles, Prayer and Hymn Books.

Oxford Bibles and Testaments.

SIZES OF TYPE.

DIAMOND.
Whatsoever ye would that men should do to you, do ye even so to them.

PEARL.
Whatsoever ye would that men should do to you, do ye even so to

RUBY.
Whatsoever ye would that men should do to you, do ye ev

NONPAREIL.
Whatsoever ye would that men should do to you, do

MINION.
Whatsoever ye would that men should do to yo

EMERALD.
Whatsoever ye would that men should do to

BREVIER.
Whatsoever ye would that men should do to

BOURGEOIS.
Whatsoever ye would that men should

LONG PRIMER.
Whatsoever ye would that men should

SMALL PICA.
Whatsoever ye would that men sho

PICA.
Whatsoever ye would that

Pearl, 24mo, cloth, gilt edges, maps, without
   Psalms $0 25
Diamond, 32mo, morocco, yapped, pocket size .. 0 50
Ruby, 32mo, morocco, yapped, without Psalms .. 0 50
Diamond, 32mo, morocco, yapped, kid lined,
   pocket size 0 75
Ruby, 16mo, morocco, yapped, reference maps,
   without Psalms 0 75
Diamond, 32mo, morocco, yapped, kid lined,
   pocket size 1 00
Ruby, 24mo, morocco, yapped, kid lined, refer-
   ences 1 00
Brilliant, 48mo, morocco, yapped, reference,
   pocket size 1 00
Pearl, 16mo, morocco, yapped, maps, reference,
   concordance, without Psalms 1 00
Brilliant, 48mo, morocco, yapped, reference, kid
   lined, India paper, pocket size 1 25
Ruby, 16mo, morocco, yapped, reference maps,
   kid lined, without Psalms 1 25
Ruby, 16mo, morocco, yapped, maps, without
   Psalms, teachers' edition 1 25
Ruby, 24mo, morocco, yapped, maps, kid lined,
   references, without Psalms, teachers' edition 1 50
Emerald, 16mo, morocco, yapped, reference
   maps, teachers' edition 1 50
Brevier, 16mo, morocco, yapped 1 50
Emerald, 16mo, morocco, yapped, kid lined, ref-
   erences 1 50
Ruby, 16mo, morocco, yapped, maps, references,
   without Psalms, teachers' edition, kid lined.. 1 75
Long primer, 16mo, morocco, yapped 1 75
Emerald, 16mo, morocco, yapped, maps, kid lined,
   references, without Psalms, teachers' edition 2 00
Emerald, 16mo, morocco, yapped, maps, refer-
   ences. Egyptian seal, without Psalms, teach-
   ers' edition, India paper 2 50
Small pica, 8vo, morocco, kid lined 2 25
Minion, 8vo, morocco, yapped, kid lined, refer-
   ence, concordance 3 00
Ruby, 16mo, Alaska seal, yapped, reference, concordance 3 00
Long primer, 8vo, India paper, kid lined, silk
   sewn, reference, teachers' edition 3 75
Minion, India paper, kid lined, levant silk sewn,
   reference 4 00
Bourgeois, India paper, kid lined, levant silk
   sewn, reference 4 25
Minion, India paper, 1-inch margin, kid lined,
   levant, reference 6 00

Family Bibles.

Sizes 11 by 13 inches,

Padded leather cover, self-pronouncing edition,
   containing the Authorized and Revised Versions of Old and New Testaments, arranged
   in parallel columns, with illustrations, and
   family record, marriage certificate, etc.,
   $3.75 to $4 50
Padded maroon leather, embossed cover, round
   corners, self-pronouncing edition, containing
   parallel columns of Authorized and Revised
   Versions of Old and New Testaments, with
   numerous Biblical illustrations, family record,
   marriage certificate, etc., $5.00 to 6 50
Padded morocco cover, red under gold edges,
   self-pronouncing edition, with numerous full-
   page, colored illustrations; also the Hofmann
   Gallery of original New Testament illustrations, with parallel columns of Authorized
   and Revised Versions of Old and New Testaments, family record, marriage certificate, etc 7 00

Prayer Books.

Prayer books, 20c, 25c, 35c, 50c, 65c
75c, 85c, $1.00.
Family prayer books, size 10½ x 8.
Illustrated, $1.50.

Prayer and Hymns Combined.

Prayer and Hymns Combined, 25c,
35c, 40c, 50c, 75c, 85c.

Hymn Books, A. and M.

Hymn books, A. and M., 25c, 35c, 50c;
large type, leather, $1.35.

Catholic Prayer Books

Sell at 15c, 30c, 40c, 45c, 50c, 65c, 75c,
$1.00, $1.25.

Testaments.

Cloth, 10c, 15c; morocco, kid lined,
50c.

Methodist Hymns.

Pearl type, size 6 x 4½.

Cloth, sprinkled edges, 25c.
Roan,   "   "   40c.
Morocco, limp, gilt edge, 65c.
   "   "   "   yapped, 75c.
   "   " leatherlined, yapped,
$1.35.

Brevier type, 7¼ x 5¼.

Cloth, sprinkled edges, 55c.
French morocco, limp, $1.10.
Persian morocco, yapped, kid lined,
$1.85.

Brevier type, 5¼ x 3¼.

Roan limp, gilt edge, $1.10.
Egyptian seal, gilt edge, yapped,
$1.35.
Persian morocco, leather lined, $1.60.

Small pica type, 6½ x 4½.

Cloth, sprinkled edges, 75c.
Persian morocco, yapped, kid lined,
$1.85.

Old People's Size—Pica type;
size, 7¼ x 5¼.

Egyptian seal, yapped, leather lined,
$2.60.

Methodist Hymns with Music.

Cloth, 90c, $1.25.
Morocco, yapped, $1.85.

Sacred Songs and Solos.

750 pieces, complete, by Ira D. San-
key, music and words—
HH 1. Cloth limp, 65c.
HH 2. Board cover, music, 85c.
FF 1. Cloth limp, large type, $1.00.
FF 2. Cloth boards, large type, $1.15.
FF 3. Bevelled boards, gilt edges,
$1.35.
AA. Words only, 90c per doz.
BB 1.   "   "   12½c each.
EE 2.   "   "   large type, 60c each.

Hymns, Ancient and Modern.

Hymns, Ancient and Modern, with
tunes, leather cover, $1.00, 1.25.
Cloth cover, 70c, $1.25.
Canadian Hymnal, with music, 45c.
   "   " words only, 10c.
   "   " cloth cover, 60c.
Finest of the Wheat, No. 1, 35c.
   "   "   " No. 2, 35c.
   "   "   " Nos. 1 and 2
combined, 50c.
The Great Redemption. John
Whyte. Paper, 20c.
The Great Redemption. John
Whyte. Limp cloth, 30c.
Triumphant Songs, No. 1, board
cover, 35c.
Triumphant Songs, No. 2, board
cover, 35c.
Triumphant Songs, No. 3, board
cover, 35c.
Triumphant Songs, No. 4, board
cover, 35c.
Triumphant Songs, Nos. 1 and 2,
combined, 60c.

New Presbyterian Hymn Books.

Ruby, 24mo.

No. 100. Black cloth, cut flush, red
edges, 10c.
No. 101. Cloth, bevelled boards, gilt
edges, gilt lettered side, 20c.
No. 111. Paste grain, limp, gilt edges,
35c.
No. 121. Venetian Rutland, limp,
round corners, red and gilt edges,
50c.

No. 109. French Rutland, yapped,
round corners, red and gilt edges,
60c.
No. 119. Paste grain, yapped, round
corners, gilt edges, 75c.
No. 139. Arabian morocco, yapped,
leather-lined, round corners, red
and gilt edges, $1.00.

Long Primer Type.

No. 200. Black cloth, red edges, 30c.
No. 201. Cloth, bevelled boards, gilt
edges, 50c.
No. 211. Paste grain, limp, gilt edges,
75c.
No. 221. Venetian rutland, limp,
round corners, gilt edges, $1.00.
P209. French seal, yapp, red and
gilt edges, $1.25.

Pica Type.

No. 300. Black cloth, red edges, 60c.
No. 311. Paste grain, gilt edges, $1.25

Hymns with Tunes.

No. 500. Cloth, 90c.
No. 501. Cloth, leather back, red
edges, $1.25.

Bibles and Hymns Combined.

Pearl Type.

P1009. French rutland, yapp, 70c.
P1010. French rutland, yapp, padded
80c.
P1020. Paste grain, yapp, padded,
90c.

Ruby Type.

P1209. French rutland, yapp, $1.00.
P1709. French rutland, references,
yapp, $1.25.
P1730. Alaska seal, references,
leather lined, $1.75.
A1759. Alaska seal, references,
leather lined, silk sewn, $3.00

Long Primer Type.

A1959. Alaska seal, yapp, leather
lined, silk sewn, references, red
and gilt edges, $6.00.

Pelonbet's Notes on International
S. S. Lessons for 1898, $1.08.

Two-Volume Sets in Half-Calf Bindings. Price, $2.25 per Set.

By Thomas Carlyle—
French Revolution, The, Vol. I.
"   "   " Vol. II.
By R. W. Emerson—
Essays, Vol. I.
"   Vol. II.
By Justin McCarthy—
History of Our Own Times, A, Vol. I.
History of Our Own Times, A, Vol. II.

Popular Sets, Bound in Half-Calf.

Charles Dickens Complete Works, 15 vols	$13 50
Scotts' Waverley Novels, 12 vols	9 60
Lytton, Bulwer, Novels, complete, 13 vols	14 50
Ruskin, John, complete, 13 vols	15 00
Carlyle, Thomas, complete, 10 vols	11 75
Cooper's Leather Stocking Tales, 5 vols	4 00

New "Popular" Sets.

The volumes in these sets are all printed on fine book paper, from large, clear type. Bound in cloth, with titles in gold stamped on the back.

Dickens, Charles, complete, 15 vols	$6 25
Carlyle, Thomas, 10 vols	6 75
Lytton, Lord, 13 vols	6 00
Eliot, George, 6 vols	2 50
Scott, Sir Walter, Waverley Novels, 12 vols	5 75
Thackeray, William M., 10 vols	4 60
Macaulay's Essays and Poems, 3 vols	1 50
Josephus' History of the Jews, 3 vols	1 85
McCarthy, Justin, History of Our Own Times, 2 vols	1 25

Standard Sets.

Ruskin, John, complete works, 10 vols	10 50
Kingsley, Rev. Charles, 8 vols	6 00
Parkman's Works, complete, 13 vols	15 00
Chambers' Encyclopædia, 12 vols	5 25

New Popular Five-volume Sets.

The titles and authors in these sets are selected for their popularity. Printed on fine book paper, in large clear type. Bound in silk corded cloth, and stamped with attractive design on back.

Cooper's Leather Stocking Tales	$2 00
Cooper's Sea Tales	2 00
Doyle, A. Conan	2 50
Gibbons' History of Rome	2 25
Green's History of England	2 25
Hawthorne, Nathaniel	2 00
Lyall, Edna	2 50
Macaulay's History of England	2 00
Ruskin's Modern Painters	2 75

New Popular Two-Volume Sets.

Uniformly bound in art linen cloth, and stamped in gold. Neatly boxed.

Price, 90c.

By Thomas Carlyle—
French Revolution, Vol. I.
"   "   Vol. II.
By R. W. Emerson—
Essays, First Series.
"   Second "
By Thomas Hughes—
Tom Brown's School Days.
Tom Brown at Oxford.
By William H. Prescott—
Conquest of Peru, Vol. I.
"   "   Vol. II.
Conquest of Mexico, Vol. I.
"   "   Vol. II.
Ferdinand and Isabella, Vol. I.
"   "   Vol. II.
By Victor Hugo—
Les Miserables, Vol. I.
"   "   Vol. II.

New Aldine Sets.

Macaulay's History of England, 5 vols	$1 35
Hawthorne's Works, 5 vols	1 35
Doyle, Conan, 5 vols	1 35
Dumas, Alexander, 8 vols	2 00

Aldine. Two-Volume Sets.

Price, 60c. per Set.

By Emerson—
Essays, First Series.
"   Second "
By Eugene Sue—
Mysteries of Paris, Vol. I.
"   "   Vol. II.
Wandering Jew, Vol. I.
"   "   Vol. II.
By Alexander Dumas—
Count of Monte Cristo, Vol. I.
"   "   Vol. II.

Miscellaneous Sets.

Rosa Nouchette Carey, 5 vols.	$1 00
Edna Lyall, 6 vols	1 25
Cooper's Leather Stocking Tales, 5 vols.	1 00
Cooper's Sea Tales, 5 vols	1 00
George Eliot, 6 vols	1 50
Dickens' Works, 15 vols.	5 50
Scott's Waverley Novels 12 vols	5 00
Lytton, Bulwer, Novels, 13 vols	5 25
Thackeray, William, 10 vols.	3 85
Guizot's History of France, 8 vols	9 00
Marie Corelli, 5 vols	$1 00
Macaulay's Essays and Poems, 3 vols	1 00
Macaulay's History of England, 5 vols	1 00
Ruskin, 4 vols	1 00
Conan Doyle, 5 vols	1 00
Smiles' Self-Help Series, 4 vols	1 00
O. W. Holmes' Breakfast Table Series, 3 vols	1 00
Napier's Peninsular War, 5 vols	2 50
Farrar's Life of Christ, 5 vols.	1 50
Shakespeare. Notes by Hudson, 12 vols	7 50
Handy Volume Shakespeare. 15 vols	3 50

"Bedford's" edition of Shakespeare's Works, 12 vols., size
32 mo., handsomely bound in
leather, good clear type, put
up in a neat leather case..... 9 50
Hawthorne. Handy Volume
Edition, 5 vols 1 25

Three-Volume Sets.

In uniform design of binding, and
boxed to match binding.

Regular price, $1.25; our price, 85c.

By R. W. Emerson—
  Essays, First Series.
   "   Second   "
By John Ruskin—
  Crown of Wild Olives, and 2 other
  selections.
By Tennyson—
  Idyls of the King.
  In Memoriam.
  The Princess and Maud.
By Longfellow—
  The Belfry of Burges, and other
  poems.
  Evangeline.
  Voices of the Night, and other
  poems.

Divinity Classics. Two Volume Sets.

Dainty little sets in exquisite
uniform bindings, and attractively
boxed to match binding.

Publisher's price, 75c.; our price, 50c.

Kept for the Master's Use. Haver-
gal.
My King and His Service. Haver-
gal.
Imitation of Christ. Thomas A'-
Kempis.
My Point of View. Drummond.
Addresses by Brooks.
   "   "   Drummond.
Steps Into the Blessed Life. F. B.
Meyer.
The Throne of Grace. F. B. Meyer.

Altemus Laurel Series.

Handsomely printed on fine laid
paper. Handy volume size. Sold
only in two volume sets.

Publisher's price, 75c.; our price, 50c. set.

Emerson's Essays, First and Second
Series.
Poems of O. W. Holmes—
  Autocrat at Breakfast Table.
My King and His Service.
Kept for the Master's Use.
Evangeline.
Marmion.
Crown of Wild Olives.
The Queen of the Air.
The Princess and Maud.
Idyls of the King.
A Window in Thrums.
Rab and His Friends.

The Canterbury Poets.

Cloth; regular price, 35c; our
price, 25c.

Longfellow.	Whitman.
Wordsworth.	Moore.
Whittier.	Southey.
Poe.	Goethe's Faust.
Burns' Poems.	Owen Meredith.
Shakespeare.	Canadian Poems.
Emerson.	Jacobite Songs.

Cabinet Poets.
Crown 8vo.

Cloth, gilt, regular price, 70c; our
price, 45c.

Shakespeare.	Wordsworth.
Longfellow.	Hemans, Mrs.
Byron.	Shelley.
Scott.	Campbell.
Burns.	Keats.
Moore.	Coleridge.
Cowper.	Goldsmith.
Milton.	R. Browning.
Whittier.	
Browning, Mrs. E. B.	

Red Line Poets.

Elegantly printed in large, clear
type.
Large crown 8vo.

Cloth, gilt, regular price, $1.25;
our price, 75c.

Longfellow.	Hemans, Mrs.
Scott.	Moore.
Milton.	Whittier.
Wordsworth.	Browning, Mrs.
Burns.	Shakespeare.
Shelley.	Byron.

Lansdowne Edition.

Padded Paste Grain; regular price,
$1.50; our price, $1.00.

Shakespeare.	Wordsworth.
Longfellow.	Byron.
Scott	Keats.
Burns.	Coleridge.
Moore.	Whittier.
Cowper.	Milton.
Browning, Mrs. E. B.	
	Goldsmith.

Lansdowne Edition.

Padded seal; regular price, $2.00;
our price, $1.50.

Lowell.	Wordsworth.
Shakespeare.	Scott.
Moore.	Longfellow.
Milton.	Burns.
Whittier.	Hemans, Mrs.

Albion Poets.

Elegantly printed in large, clear
type.
Large crown 8vo.
Padded Nubian, regular, $2.50
our price, $2.00.

Shakespeare.	Whittier.
Longfellow.	Wordsworth.
Scott.	Burns.
Milton.	Byron.
Moore.	

Albion Edition.

Padded seal; regular price, $3.00;
our price, $2.25.

Shakespeare.	Scott.
Longfellow.	Burns.
Moore.	Whittier.
Wordsworth.	Byron.

Tennyson's Poems.

Tennyson, cloth		$1 00
"	paste grain leather	1 50
"	padded morocco do	2 00
"	" " do complete	2 50
"	padded paste grain lea her complete	3 00
"	padded seal leather, complete	3 50

Half Levant Leather Edition.
Printed on Fine Paper.
Size 16mo.

Publisher's price, 70c; our price, 50c
The Lady of the Lake. Sir Walter
  Scott.
Marmion. Sir Walter Scott.
Mosses from an Old Manse. Haw-
  thorne.
Twice Told Tales. Hawthorne.
Modern Painters. Ruskin.
Crown of Wild Olives. Ruskin.
Queen of the Air. Ruskin.
Stones of Venice. Ruskin.
The Princess. Tennyson.
Idyls of the King. Tennyson.
Tales from Shakespeare. Lamb.
Dreams. Olive Schreigner.
Natural Law in Spiritual World
  Drummond.
Addresses. Drummond.
Light of Asia. Arnold.
Reveries of a Bachelor. Ik. Marvel.
Lucile. Owen Meredith.
Vicar of Wakefield. Goldsmith.
Childe Harold, a Pilgrimage. Byron.
Brooks Addresses.

Altemus Representative Poets.

Handsomely printed on fine laid
paper, from clear, open-faced type,
and beautifully bound in handy
volume size. Cloth, new and original design, gilt top.

Publisher's price, 50c.; our price, 35c.

Marmion. Sir Walter Scott.
The Lady of The Lake. Sir Walter
  Scott.
The Last Leaf, and other poems. O.
  W. Holmes.
Lalla Rookh. Thomas Moore.
The Light of Asia. Edwin Arnold.
Poems. James Russell Lowell.
Ballads. Rudyard Kipling.
In Memoriam. Tennyson.

The World Library.

Bound in blue and grey cloth.
Regular price, $1.25; our price, 85c.
Plutarch's Lives.
Whiston's Josephus.
Bacon's Essays.
Hume's Essays.

Adam Smith's Wealth of Nations.
Hallam's Europe.
Essays. Thomas de Quincey.
Locke's Human Understanding.
D'Aubigne's Reformation.

S. R. Crockett's Works.

Men of the Moss-Haggs.	Cloth	$1 00
" "	Paper	0 65
The Raiders. Cloth		1 00
The Stickit Minister. Cloth		1 00
Cleg Kelly. Paper		0 45
" Cloth		1 00
Lilac Sunbonnet. Paper		0 60
" " Cloth		0 90
The Gray Man. Cloth		0 90
The Gray Man. Paper		0 65
Lad's Love. Paper		0 65
" " Cloth		0 90

Works by Marie Corelli.

Barabbas. Paper		$0 65
Sorrows of Satan. Paper		0 65
" " Cloth		0 90
The Mighty Atom. Paper		0 65
" " Cloth		0 90
The Murder of Delicia. Cloth.		0 90
The Murder of Delicia. Paper.		0 65
Barabbas. Cloth		0 90
Ziska. Paper		0 65
" Cloth		0 90

Jan Maclaren's Works.

CLOTH.

Beside the Bonnie Brier Bush	$0 90
The Days of Auld Lang Syne	0 90
The Mind of the Master	1 00
The Upper Room	0 45
Kate Carnegie	1 00
The Cure of Souls	1 00
Beside the Bonnie Brier Bush. Paper	0 43
The Days of Auld Lang Syne, paper	0 43
Kate Carnegie, paper	0 43

Miscellaneous and New Books.

Shakespeare, large type, cloth	$0 75
Black Beauty. A. Sewell. "	0 45
Beautiful Joe. M. Saunders. Paper	0 24
Beautiful Joe. M. Saunders. Cloth	0 65
Lion, the Mastiff. A. G. Savigny. Cloth	0 50
Electricity up to Date. Cloth	0 45
Little Lord Fauntleroy. Mrs. Burnett. Cloth	0 85
A House-Boat on the Styx. Bangs. Cloth	0 60
A House-Boat on the Styx. Bangs. Cloth	1 10
The Pursuit of the House-Boat. Bangs. Cloth	1 10
Successward. Ed. W. Bok. Cloth	0 80
The Seats of the Mighty. Gilbert Parker. Paper	0 65
The Seats of the Mighty. Gilbert Parker. Cloth	1 00
The Pomp of the Lavilettes. Gilbert Parker. Cloth	1 00
The Exploits of Brigadier Gerard. Conan Doyle Cloth	0 90
Rodney Stone. Doyle. Cloth	0 90
" " " Paper	0 65

A Night of the Nets. A. E. Barr. Cloth	$1 00
God's Winepress. A. Jenkinson. Cloth	0 75
Heather from the Brae. David Lyatt. Cloth	0 65
Margaret Ogilvy. Barrie. Cloth	1 10
Sentimental Tommy. Barrie. Cloth	0 90
Sentimental Tommy. Barrie. Paper	0 65
A Rebellious Heroine. Bangs. Cloth	1 10
Seven Seas. Kipling. Paper	0 65
" " " Cloth	0 90
Havergal's Poems. 3 vols., boxed, cloth	1 35
Havergal's complete Prose Works. 1 vol., cloth	1 25
Constitutional History of England. Hallam. Cloth	0 75
The Sowers. Merriman. Paper	0 65
" " Cloth	1 10
Flotsam. " Paper	0 65
" " Cloth	1 00
With Edged Tools. Merriman. Cloth	1 10
Cruden's Concordance. Cloth.	0 75
Gold Dust	0 35
Farthest North. By Nansen. 2 vols., paper, $1.30; cloth	1 85
Temple edition of Shakespeare, each play bound in separate volume, cloth edition, gilt top	0 30
Leather edition, gilt top	0 45
Chambers' Concise Gazetteer of the World	1 40
Phroso. Anthony Hope. Cloth	1 00
Shakespeare. Cloth	0 20
Soldiers of Fortune. Richard Harding Davis. Paper	0 65
Soldiers of Fortune. Richard Harding Davis. Cloth	1 10
Quo Vadis. A Narrative of Rome at the Time of Nero. Cloth	1 50
The Wrestler of Philippi. Fanny E. Newberry. Paper	0 10
The Wrestler of Philippi. Fanny E. Newberry. Cloth	0 35
The Physical Life of Woman. Dr. Napheys. Cloth	0 80
The Transmission of Life. Dr. Napheys. Cloth	0 80
Tokology. Alice B. Stockham	2 75
Equality. Edward Bellamy. Paper	0 65
Equality. Edward Bellamy. Cloth	1 10
The Martian. By Du Maurier. Paper, 65c; cloth	1 00
Chevalier D'Auriac. By S. L. Yeats. Paper	0 65
The Christian. By Hall Caine. Paper, 65c; cloth	1 35
In Kedar's Tents. By Merriman. Paper	0 65
The Pursuit of the House Boat. By Bangs. Cloth	0 60
On the Face of the Waters. By F. A. Steel. Paper, 65c; Cloth	1 00
A History of Our Own Times from 1880 to Diamond Jubilee. By Justin McCarthy. Cloth.	1 50
Guesses at the Riddle of Existence. By Goldwin Smith. Cloth	1 15
The Old Testament Vindicated. By G. C. Workman. Cloth.	0 55

The Grey Lady. By H. S. Merriman, cloth	$1 25
The Choir Invisible. By James Lane Allen, cloth	1 25
Ascent of Man. By Drummond, cloth	1 65
Cursed by a Fortune. By Manville Fenn, cloth	0 90
Probable Sons. By author of Teddy's Buttons, cloth	0 30

Henty Books for Boys.

CLOTH, ILLUSTRATED.

Regular price, $1.75; our price, $1.15.

A Knight of the White Cross.
The Tiger of Mysore.
When London Burned.
In the Heart of the Rockies.
Beric, the Briton.
By Right of Conquest.
In Greek Waters.
Redskin and Cowboy.
The Dash for Khartoum.
Condemned as a Nihilist; A Tale of Escape from Siberia.
Held Fast for England; A Tale of Gibraltar.
St. Bartholomew's Eve.
Maori and Settler.
Thro' Russian Snows.
On the Irrawaddy.
Wulf the Saxon.
At Agincourt.
With Cochrane the Dauntless.
Moore at Corunna.
March on London.
With Frederick the Great.

Henty Books.

Regular price, $1.00; our price, 70c.

Bonnie Prince Charlie.
By England's Aid.
By Pike and Dyke.
In Freedom's Cause.
The Young Carthaginians.
The Dragon and the Raven.
With Clive in India.
With Lee in Virginia.
Captain Bayley's Heir.
The Lion of the North.
Under Drake's Flag.
In the Reign of Terror.
True to the Old Flag.
With Wolfe in Canada.
By Right of Conquest.

St. George for England.
The Bravest of the Brave.
For Name and Fame.
The Cat of Bubastes.
For the Temple.
The Lion of St. Mark.
By Sheer Pluck.
A Final Reckoning.
Facing Death.
Maori and Settler.

Works by Jackson Wray.

CLOTH.

Regular price, $1.25 ; our price, 75c.

Old Crusty's Niece.
Betwixt Two Fires.
Light from the Old Lamp.
Garton Rowley.
Honest John Stallibrass.
Mathew Mellowdew.
Nestleton Magna.
A Man Every Inch of Him.

Works by Silas Hocking.

CLOTH.

Regular price, 75c.; our price, 55c.

Her Benny : A Story of Street Life.
Ivy : A Tale of Cottage Life.
His Father ; or, A Mother's Legacy.
Alec. Green : A Tale of Sea Life.
Cricket : A Tale of Humble Life.
Crookleigh : A Village Story.
Real Grit.
Rex Raynor.
Doctor Dick.
Chips : Joe and Mike.

Star Series.

CLOTH.

Regular price, 70c ; our price, 45c.

Drayton Hall. Alice Gray.
By E. Wetherell—
Say and Seal.
Golden Ladder.
Vinegar Hill.
What She Could.
Wych Hazel.
Gold of Chickaree.
Diana.
The Letter of Credit.
The End of a Coil.
My Desire.
Nobody.
Little Women and Little Wives.
Alcott.
Without and Within. W. Jay.
Sceptres and Crowns, etc.
Little Sunbeams. J. H. Mathews.
Ben Hur. Lew Wallace.
By A. E. Barr—
A Daughter of Fife.
The Bow of Orange Ribbon.
Between Two Loves.
Englefield Grange. H. B. Paull.
Leyton Auberry's Daughters.

Works by Florence M. Kingsley.

Titus.	Paper	$0 10
"	Cloth	0 35
"	"	0 80
Stephen.	Paper	0 35
"	Cloth	0 65
Paul.	Paper	0 40
"	Cloth	0 85

Devotional Series.

Full white vellum, handsome and appropriate design in silver and monotint, boxed.

Publisher's price, 50c; our price, 35c.

Kept for the Master's Use. Frances Ridley Havergal.
My King and His Service. Frances Ridley Havergal.
My Point of View. Selections from Drummond's Works.
Of the Imitation of Christ. Thomas a Kempis.
Addresses. Henry Drummond.
Natural Law in the Spiritual World. Henry Drummond.
Addresses. Rt. Rev. Phillips Brooks.
Steps into the Blessed Life. Rev. F. B. Meyer.
John Ploughman's Talks. Rev. Charles Spurgeon.
The Changed Cross.
The Christian Life. Rev. A. Oxenden.

Young People's Library.

Publisher's price, 50c; our price, 30c.

A new series of choice literature for children, selected from the best and most popular works. Handsomely printed on fine super-calendered paper from large clear type and profusely illustrated by the most famous artists, making the handsomest and most attractive series of juvenile classics before the public. In a uniform size—square 16mo.
The Adventures of Robinson Crusoe. (70 illustrations.)
Alice's Adventures in Wonderland. (42 illustrations.)
Through the Looking Glass and What Alice Found There. (50 illustrations.)
The Story of Exploration and Adventure in Africa.
Bunyan's Pilgrim's Progress. (46 illustrations.)
A Child's Story of the Bible. (72 illustrations.)

A Child's Life of Christ. (49 illustrations.)
Æsop's Fables. (62 illustrations.)

Swiss Family Robinson. (50 illustrations.)
Christopher Columbus and the Discovery of America. (70 illustrations.)
Gulliver's Travels. (50 illustrations.)
Mother Goose's Rhymes, Jingles and Stories. (234 illustrations.)
The Story of the Frozen Seas. (70 illustrations.)
Wood's Natural History. (80 illustrations.)
Arabian Nights. 110 illustrations.

Works of Andrew Murray.

CLOTH.

Jesus Himself	$0 30
Love Made Perfect	0 30
The Spirit of Christ	0 40
The Master's Indwelling	0 40
Holy in Christ	0 40

Illustrated Vade Mecum Series.

Each volume contains illuminated title and portrait of author and illustrations in monochrome tints. Full cloth, ivory finish, ornamental inlaid back and side, boxed.

Publisher's price, 40c; our price, 25c.

Ethics of the Dust. John Ruskin.
Pleasures of Life. Sir John Lubbock.
Scarlet Letter. Nathaniel Hawthorne.
House of the Seven Gables. Nathaniel Hawthorne.
Mosses from an Old Manse. Nathaniel Hawthorne.
Twice Told Tales. Nathaniel Hawthorne.
Bacon's Essays.
Representative Men. Ralph Waldo Emerson.
The Light of Asia. Sir Edwin Arnold.
The Lays of Ancient Rome. T. B. Macaulay.
Thoughts of Marcus Aurelius.
Imitation of Christ. Thos. a Kempis.
Addresses. Henry Drummond.
Reveries of a Bachelor. Ik Marvel.
Dream Life. Ik Marvel.
Sartor Resartus. Thomas Carlyle.
Heroes and Hero Worship. Thomas Carlyle.
My Point of View. Selections from Drummond's Works.
Sketch Book. Washington Irving.
Kept for the Master's Use. Frances Ridley Havergal.
Lucile. Owen Meredith.
Lalla Rookh. Thomas Moore.
Lady of the Lake. Sir Walter Scott.
Marmion. Sir Walter Scott.
Princess. Alfred, Lord Tennyson.
Idylls of the King. Alfred, Lord Tennyson.
Evangeline. Henry W. Longfellow.
The Queen of the Air.
Greek Heroes. Charles Kingsley.
A Wonder Book. Nathaniel Hawthorne.
Addresses by Phillips Brooks.
The Crown of Wild Olive. John Ruskin.
Natural Law in the Spiritual World. Henry Drummond.

Claremont Series.

Handsomely bound in cloth. Illustrated.

Regular price, 50c ; our price, 25c.

By A. L. O. E.—
Tho Claremont Tales.
A Wreath of Smoke.
Grace Vernon.
Christian Conquests.
The Lake of the Woods.
Little Bullets from Batalo.
Seven Perils Passed.
The Battle of Life.
The Wondrous Sickle.
Tales Illustrative of the Parables.
Jack Roden. William Martin.
By W. H. G. Kingston—
Happy Jack.
Archie Hughson.
Uncle Boz.
Waihoura.
Janet Maclaren.
The Ocean and Its Wonders.
The Mine   "   "
The African Trader.
By Ascott R. Hope—
The Volcano and Its Wonders.
Electricity. Illustrated.
Old Carroll's Will. S. G. Goodrich.
In the Service. Isabel Hornibrook.

Cook Books.

Mrs. Beeton's Book of Household Management. Cloth...	$1 75
Century Cook Book............	1 90
Miss Parloa's Young Housekeeper......................	1 00
Miss Parloa's New Cook Book and Marketing Guide	1 25
Home Cook Book	0 50
Dr. Chase's New Receipt Book	0 50
Mrs. Rorer's Cook Book	1 45

Elocution Books.

Little People's Speaker, 15c.
Young Folk's Recitations, 15c.
Child's Own Speaker, 15c.
Shoemaker's Best Selections, Nos. 1 to 23, 25c. each.
Wilson's Recitations and Dialogues, 25c.
Dick's Comic Dialogues, 25c.
Choice Dialogues, 25c.
Young Folks Dialogues 25c.
McBride's Choice Dialogues, 25c.
Kavanaugh's New Speeches and Dialogues for Children, 25c.

Annuals.

Chums......................	$2 00
Boy's Own	1 65
Girl's Own	1 65
Sunday at Home..............	1 50
Leisure Hours.................	1 50
Cassels Family Magazine, Cloth	0 75

Juvenile Books.

Young People's Pilgrims Progress, with complete account of Life of John Bunyan, Illustrated. Cloth, 55c.
Bible Talks in Simple Language, especially adapted to the young. Illustrated. Cloth cover, 65c.

Toy and Picture Books.

POSTPAID.

2c. each.

6 Assorted titles, shaped.

5c. each.

Mother Goose's Melodies,
Noah's Ark.
Kriss Kringle Series.
Pearl Series.
Mistletoe Series.

8c. each.

Topsy Series, shaped.
Tea Party Series, shaped.
Simple Simon.
Ten Little Niggars.
Jack and the Bean Stalk.
The Robber Within.

10c. each.

Mother Goose.
Kriss Kringle.
Goody Two Shoes.
Little Bo-Peep.

15c. each.

Doings of Kriss Kringle.
Apple Pie A B C.
Baby's A B C.
Robinson Crusoe.
Mother Goose's Chimes.

20c. each.

Circus and Menagerie A B C.
Home Animals.
Humpty Dumpty.
Boy's Hunting Book.
Little Folks Pleasures.

Painting Books.

Little Folks, 10c.
New Palette, 15c.
Ideal, 25c.

Linen Books.

Little Daylight, 5c.
Red Riding Hood, 10c.
Little Pets, 10c.
Kriss Kringle, 10c.
Little Folks, 20c.
Noah's Ark, 20c.
Mother Goose, 25c.
Little Pig, 25c.
Cock Robin, 30c.
Mother Goose 30c.

Illustrated Board Covers.

Santa Clause Series, 6 kinds, 10c ea., postage 3c extra.
Jack Frost Series, 6 kinds, 12c ea., postage, 4c extra.
Happy Hour Series, 4 kinds, 15c ea., postage, 5c extra.
Story Land Series, 4 kinds, 20c ea., postage, 7c extra.
Chit Chat Series, 4 kinds, 25c ea., postage 8c extra.
Stories and Pictures from Old Testament, by Pansy, 25c ea., postage, c5 extra.
Stories and Pictures from New Testament, by Pansy, 25c ea., postage 5c extra.

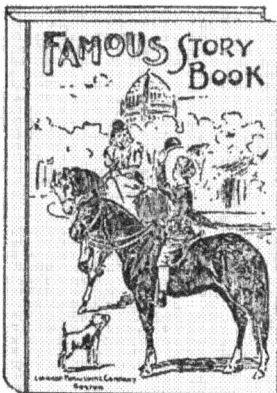

Famous Story Book, with colored frontispiece, 50c ea., postage, 10c extra.

The Sunday Book, by Pansy, with colored frontispiece, 50c ea., postage, 10c extra.

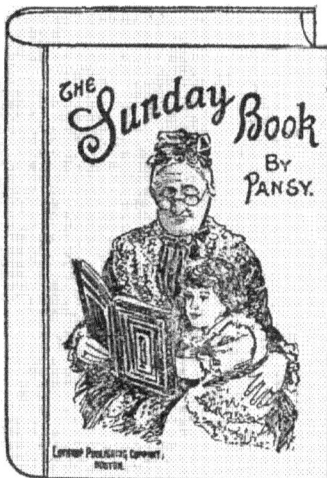

The Pansy Book, with colored frontispiece, 65c ea., postage, 10c. extra.
Animal Story Book, colored frontispiece, 60c ea., postage, 10c extra.
Boys' Book of Adventures, colored frontispiece, 50c ea., postage, 10c extra.

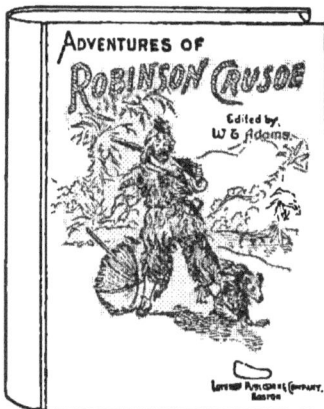

Adventures of Robinson Crusoe, colored frontispiece, 50c ea., postage, 10c extra.
Our Darlings, colored illustrations, 35c ea., postage, 10c extra.
Chatterbox, colored illustrations, 75c ea., postage, 10c extra.
Chatterbox, cloth cover, colored illustrations, $1.00 ea., postage, 10c extra.
Bible Story Book, 60c ea., postage, 10c extra.
Gospel Story Book, 60c ea., postage, 10c extra.

POSTAGE STAMP ALBUMS.

Postage Extra.

The International Postage Stamp Album, illustrated with 5,552 engravings of stamps, 160 of arms, 665 of watermarks, 70 portraits of regents, 4,433 quotations of rare stamps, with one map, $1.50.

The International Postage Stamp Album, published in three languages, providing for 11,082 postage stamps, cards, envelopes, etc., with one map, $1.00.

The International Postage Stamp Album, providing for 4,500 postage stamps, cards, envelopes, etc., 50c.

Illustrated Postage Stamp Album, with 2,139 engravings of stamps, 79 arms and 49 portraits, 35c.

Illustrated Postage Stamp Album, with 1,860 engravings of stamps, 57 watermarks, 69 arms, and 24 portraits, 25c.

SCRAP ALBUMS.

Postage Extra.

Scrap Albums, bound in cloth, 30c, 35c, 50c each.
Scrap Albums, board covers, 20c, 25c each.

PHOTOGRAPH ALBUMS.

Postage Extra.

Leather Bound Albums for 20 cabinet pictures and 16 visites, spring clasp, 75c; postage, 24c extra.

Leather Bound Albums, for 24 cabinet photos and 16 visites, spring clasp, $1.00; postage 25c extra.
Leather Albums, for 28 cabinets and 16 visites, $1.25; postage, 28c extra.

Atlases and Globes.

The Library Globe Atlas, of Ancient and Modern Geography, containing 37 quarto pages of maps, cloth cover, $1.25.
Rand and McNally's Popular Atlas of the World, cloth cover, $1.50. .
The Victoria Regina Atlas, Political, Physical, Astronomical, containing 200 plates and complete index, bound in half leather, $5.00.
12-in. full Meridian Globe, $6.25, express extra.
9-in. full Meridian Globe, $4.00, express extra.
12-in. plain Globe, $4.00, express extra.
9-in. plain Globe, $3.00, express extra.

Christmas Cards.

POSTPAID.

Christmas Cards, in packages of one dozen, 10c, 15c, 25c, 35c, 50c package.
Fancy leaflet Christmas cards, handsome designs, 5c, 8c, 10c, 12½c ea.
Fancy text cards, for Sunday school classes, etc., 10 cards in package, 10c, 15c package.

Booklets, 10c. each.

The Hundredth Psalm.
The Wind Sown Flowers.
My Thoughts.
In Sunshine Clad.
Jesus, My All.

Booklets, 15c. each.

The First Flowers.
Sweet Memories.
Murmured Through the Holly Branches.

Booklets, 20c. each.

The Angelus.
The Mystery of God's Love.
Christmas Hymn.
A Song From the Heart.
One, and then Another.

Booklets, 25c. each.

I Know That My Redeemer Liveth.
Jesus, Saviour, Pilot Me.
Under the Open Sky.
Day Unto Day.
Hark, the Herald Angel Sings.
We Shall Be Satisfied.
Daily Strength.
The Christmas Message,

Booklets, 30c. each.

I Need Thee, lace cover.
Just As I Am, lace cover.
The Angels' Song, lace cover.
The Pathway of Peace, lace cover.
Hark, the Herald Angels Sing, lace cover.
My Birthday.

Calendars.

POSTPAID.

Block Calendars, for fancy work, 3c, 5c, 8c each.
Pocket booklet Calendars, 1c, 3c, 5c ea.
Fancy leaflet Calendars, 8c, 10c, 12½c ea.

3 Slat Drop Calendars, 10c. each.

Erica.
Primrose.
Cats and Dogs.

12 Leaf Calendars (overturn) 15c. each.

Twilight Hour, flowers and scenery.
I Need Thee,   "   "
Daily Strength.   "   "

4 Slat Drop Calendars, 20c. each.

Fond Meditation.
Merry Days.

12 Leaf Calendars (overturn) 20c. each.

Aim High.
Golden Months,
Time's Onward Tide.
Divine Guidance.
Fields and Flowers.

Drop Calendars, 25c. each.

Sunny Days.
Gems of Thought.
Remembrance.
Fragrant Flowers.
Fancy Embossed Flowers.
Gems from Rural Life.
Sacred Thoughts.
Words of Good Cheer.

Leaf Calendars (overturn) 25c. each.

Fleeting Thoughts.
Season's Greeting.
Pleasures of Youth.
Gems from Shakespeare.
Gems from Tennyson,
Gems from Whittier.
Quiet Paths.

Fancy Calendars, 25c. each.

Glad Hearts.
Sweet Solitude.
Innocent Hearts.
Sweet Marguerite.
Gathered Garlands.

Fancy Calendars, 35c. each.

Forget-Me-Not Novelty.
Good Luck.
Melodies of Thought.

Fancy Calendars, 50c. each..

The Beatitudes.
Lady of the Lake.
Evangeline.
Fancy Folding, embossed Forget.
Me-Nots.
Wayside Gatherings, violets and chrysanthemums.
Seventy-Third Psalm.
Folding Fan.
Good Luck.

Fancy Calendars, 75c. each.

Changeful Year.
Sweet Reveries.
Bells of Joy.
Golden Hours.

Fancy Calendars, $1.00.

The Minuet.
Sweet Melodies.
Large Folding Fan.

Fancy Calendars, $1.50.,

Scenes from Shakespeare.

Fancy Pencils.

Solid gold pencils, chased and plain, with slide, $2.00, 2.50, 3.00, 3.50, 4.00, 5.00, 5.50 each.
Sterling silver pencils, $1.00, 1.25, 1.50, 2.00 each.
Pearl pencils, with slide, 75c each.
Celluloid pencils, with slide, 50c each.
Fancy pencils, with slide, 10c, 15c 25c each.

Gold Pens.

Pearl handle pens, plain, with solid gold points, $1.00, 1.25, 1.50 each
Pearl handle pens, rustic, with solid gold points, $2.00, 2.25, 2.50 each.

Paper Knives.

Pearl paper knives, 25c, 35c, 50c each.
Pearl paper knives, with sterling silver handles, 25c, 35c, 65c, $1.00 each.

Fountain Pens.

Paul E. Wirt fountain pens, chased handles, solid gold points, fine or medium points, $1.75 each.
Weidlich fountain pens, chased handles, solid gold points, fine or medium points, $1.25 each.
University fountain pens, chased handles, solid gold points, fine or medium points, $1.00 each.

Papeteries.

Postage extra.

Fancy papeteries in all styles, 10c, 15c, 25c, 30c, 35c, 50c, 65c, 75c, $1.00, 1.25, 1.50 each.

Postage extra on the following:

Fine crepe tissue paper in all shades, 10c roll.

Plain tissue paper, in all shades, 20c, 30c, 40c quire.

Pencil Cases.

Postage extra on following :

Pencil cases, single slide, 3c each, postage extra, 3c.
Pencil cases, single slide, 5c each, postage extra, 3c.
Pencil cases, single slide, 10c each, postage extra, 5c.
Pencil cases, double slide, 15c each, postage extra, 6c.
Pencil cases, lock and key, 20c each, postage extra, 6c.

Household and Fancy Linens.

MANY needle women are deterred from undertaking a piece of elaborate embroidery on account of supposed inability to carry out the work in an artistic manner. The ladies of this department will obviate this difficulty and will be willing to start your embroidery at any time.

Fancy Needlework, Etc.

Hand embroidered centre pieces on fine white linen, button-hole edge, with scattered chrysanthemums, violets, holly, roses, thistles, etc., sizes 18 x 18 and 20 x 20 inches, $2.00 to 3.00 each.

Hemstitched table covers, embroidered on fine white linen, with drawn work, scattered holly and violets with large spray in corners, $2.50 to 4.00 each.

Plain hemstitched tray covers, or with fancy open work corners, embroidered on fine white linen, scattered flowers in different designs, size 20 x 30 inches, $1.50 to 3.00 each.

Hand-made Battenburg lace centre pieces, in all the very latest designs, size 20 x 20 inches, $1.00, 1.25, 1.50 and 1.75 each.

Silk sofa pillows, heavily embroidered with silk and bullion in all the new designs, finished with double china silk frill, shades olive, nile green, blue, yellow, pink and white. Down forms $3.50 to 5.00 each ; batting forms, $2.50 to 3.50 each.

Something Quite New.

Black satin sofa pillows, hand embroidered, with scattered violets, roses or any flower preferred, with frill to harmonize, pure down form, $4.50 and 5.00 each.

Toilet Cushions.

Square or round, made in all shades, with lace or embroidered tops, prettily trimmed with lace and ribbon, $1.00 to 2.50 each.

Comb and Brush Cases.

Hand embroidered with scattered flowers, finished with silk and lace, $1.25 to $2.00 ea.

Tea Cosies.

Full size tea cosies, covered with fine satins, batting form, 75c. to $1.50 each.

Fine silk tea cosies, in any shade, finished with deep silk puffing, down form, $1.50 to 2.00 ea.

Hand-embroidered tea cosies on fine white linen, scattered flowers, elaborately finished with silk puffings, pure down forms, $3.00, 3.50 and 4.00 each.

Dainty Gifts for Gentlemen.

Handkerchiefs and tie cases. These dainty cases can be used for handkerchiefs, cravats, gloves, etc. Handkerchief case is 9½ x 18 inches (closed), cravat and glove case, 6 x 18 inches (closed), embroidered on fine white linen, with scattered flowers, monograms, etc., finished with double silk frill and lace, $1.50 to 2.50 each.

Hat band initials, embroidered on 3-inch satin ribbon, richly finished, 75c each.

Bicycle ribbon initials, embroidered in club colors, two shades of ribbon, $1.00 each.

Photo frames, embroidered on fine white linen, square, round or heart shaped, conventional or floral designs, $1.00, 1.50, 2.00 each.

Crochet hair receivers, pineapple design, made of white and shaded crotchet cotton, lined with silk, finished with puffings and ribbon, 50c each.

Silk or satin sofa pillows, with hand-made Battenburg tops, silk or satin, any color to order, finished with 4-inch frill, down forms, $3.00 to 5.00 each.

Fancy silk head rests, square or diamond shape, finished with lace and ribbon, any shade required to order, 75c, to $1.50 each.

Hand-embroidered cosy sides, on our special No. 7 fine linen, embroidered in the very newest designs procurable, $1.25 to 2.50 each.

Stamped laundry bags, plain white, size 18 x 30, 25c and 30c ; 20 x 32, 30c and 35c each.

Laundry bags, plain white, with pink and blue tops, stamped for working, size 20 x 30, 35c, 40c and 50c each.

Plaid cambric cushions, white, with cardinal, blue, olive, gold and mauve plaid, embroidered with silk, finished with 4-inch frill, batting form, $1.25 each.

Denim sofa pillows, embroidered in silk or braid, size 22 x 22, with heavy 4-inch frill, batting form, $2.00 and 2.50 ; down forms, $3.00 and 3.50 each.

Art ticking cushions, blue and white, green and white, and red and white stripes, made with 4-inch frill, batting form, $1.50 each.

Tea cosy, forms Russian down, 12 x 14, 25c, 35c and 40c ; pure eiderdown, 50c and 60c ea.

Pin cushions, uncovered, all shapes and sizes, 10c each.

Christmas Linens.

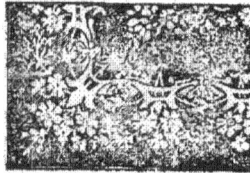

Fine bleached German damask table cloths, hemstitched, in large choice of new designs, full bleached; fine satin finish, sizes 2 x 2 yards, $1.75, 2.00 to 4.00 ; 2 x 2½ yds, $2.50, 3.00 to 7.50 ; 2 x 3 yards, $4.00, 4.50, to 8.00.

Fine bleached damask cloths, finished with border all round, Irish manufacture, superior quality in finish and bleach, No. 80, size 2 x 2½ yards, $1.25 ; No. 100, 2 x 2½ yards, $1.50 ; No. 120, 2 x 2½ yards, $1.75 ; No. 130, 2 x 2½ yards, $2.00 ; No. 140, 2 x 2½ yards, $2.25 ; No. 150, 2 x 2½ yards, $2.50.

An exceptional offer in fine bleached double damask table cloths, finished with border all round, very superior quality, guaranteed all pure linen, fine satin finish, in a choice collection of new designs—No. 141, 2 x 2½ yards, $2.00 ; No. 136, 2 x 2½ yards, $2.00 ; No. 141, 2 x 3 yards, $2.50 ; No. 136, 2 x 3, $2.50 each.

Heavy bleached double damasks, a new collection of designs, Irish and Scotch manufacture; guaranteed all pure linen, fine satin finish, full bleached—72 inches wide, 65c, 75c, 83c and $1.00 yard.

Hemstitched damask napkins, fine satin finish, German bleached, in new designs, size 20 x 20, $3.50 and 4.00 ; 21 x 21, $4.00 to 6.50 ; 23 x 23, $6.00 to 9.00.

Fine bleached damasks, guaranteed all pure linen, soft grass bleach, in new designs—62, 64, 66 inches, 40c, 45c and 50c ; 66, 68, 70 inches, 50c yard.

Fine bleached double damask napkins, superior quality, pure linen, choice range of new patterns, satin finish, size ⅝ x ⅝, $1.85, 2.00, 2.25 doz.

Fine bleached damask napkins, guaranteed all pure linen, fine satin finish, in new designs, size ¾ x ¾, $1.00, 1.25, 1.50, 1.75 doz.

Fine bleached damask napkins, superior quality, guaranteed pure linen, new patterns, size ⅝ x ⅝, $1.00, 1.25, 1.50 to 2.50 doz.

Bleached damask napkins, hemmed, ready for use, in new patterns, size ⅝ x ⅝, $1.00, 1.09, 1.19 ; ¾ x ¾, $1.00, 1.25, 1.35 to 2.00 doz.

Fine half-bleached loom damasks, in a new collection of designs, superior quality, special finished, 58, 60, 62 and 64 inches, 25c and 30c ; 64, 66, 68 and 70 inches, 35c, 40c and 50c yard.

Stamped Linens.

Stamped linen centre pieces on special fine soft finished linen, manufactured for fine art needlework in following sizes : 6 x 6, 3c, 5c ; 9 x 9, 5 c, 8 c ; 12 x 12, 8c, 10c, 12½c ; 15 x 15, 12½c, 15c. 18c ; 18 x 18, 15c, 18c, 20c ; 20 x 20, 20c, 25c, 30c ; 22 x 22, 20c, 25c, 30c each.

Hemstitched plain linens, with fancy drawn work, stamped in sprays, flowers, etc., in sideboard scarfs, 5 o'clock tea cloths, trays and pillow shams, in following sizes : 18 x 27, 25c, 30c, 35c, 40c ; 20 x 30, 25c, 35c, 45c, 50c, 60c ; 18 x 72, 60c, 75c, 85c, $1.00 1.25 ; 32 x 32, 50c, 60c, 75c, 85c, $1.00 ; 36 x 36, 60c, 75c, 85c, $1.00, 1.25 each.

Japanese Silk Drapes, Covers and Scarfs.

Japanese silk mantle or piano drapes, richly embroidered in heavy gold bullion, with deep heavy knotted silk fringe, in all shades, full size, $2.00, 2.50, 2.75, 3.00, 3.50 and 4.00 each.

Japanese silk table covers, embroidered in all the latest designs, with silk and bullion, pure Shanghai silk, heavy knotted silk fringe, all colors, size 36 x 36, $2.00, 2.50, 3.00 and 3.50 each.

Our special silk table cover, embroidered with gold bullion, in all the leading shades, heavy knotted silk fringe, size 36 x 36, $1.50 each.

Japanese silk drapes, can be used for either mantle or piano, handsomely embroidered in all the newest designs, with silk and gold thread, colors, nile, green, garnet, blue, pink, yellow or cream, fine silk fringe, size 27 x 108, special $4.00, 4.50 each.

Shanghai silk picture or easel scarfs, all colors, assorted designs, gold embroidery, with knotted silk fringe, 40c, 50c, 65c, 75c, 85c, $1.00 each.

Special Japanese silk mantle or piano drapes, embroidered with gold thread, full range of colors, heavy knotted silk fringe, full size, special $2.50 each.

Japanese silk picture or chair scarfs, real Shanghai silk, embroidered with bullion on both ends, handsome designs, size 18 x 50, special, 75c each.

Tea Cloths, Sideboard Scarfs, Tray Covers, Etc.

Fine hemstitched satin damask 5 o'clock tea cloths, large range of all the newest designs, size, 36 x 36, 75c, 85c, $1.00, 1.25, 1.50 each.

Satin damask table covers, with fancy open work and heavy knotted fringe, size 36 x 36, 65c, 75c, 85c, $1.00, 1.25 each.

Satin damask tray or carving cloths, with fancy open work and tied fringes, all new designs, stamped if required, size 20 x 30, 29c, 35c, 50c, 60c each.

Fine bleached damask sideboard scarfs, extra heavy quality, satin finish, with fancy open work and sewn fringe all around, size 18 x 72, 50c, 65c, 75c, 85c, $1.00 each.

Hemstitched satin damask sideboard scarfs, full range of all the newest patterns, size 18 x 72, 75c, 85c, $1.00, 1.25 each.

Hemstitched damask tray cloths, assorted patterns in spots, sprays and flowers, extra quality, sizes 18 x 27 and 20 x 30, 30c, 40c, 50c, 65c, 75c each.

German linen crepe sideboard scarfs with fancy open work sides and ends, knotted fringe, size 17 x 70, 30c, 35c, 40c, 50c, 65c each.

Plain white linen hemstitched sideboard scarfs, with fancy open-work corners, extra quality, size 18 x 72, 50c, 65c, 75c, $1.00, 1.25 each.

Hemstitched and drawn plain linen 5 o'clock tea cloths, fine quality, size 36 x 36, 60c. 75c, 85c, $1.00 each.

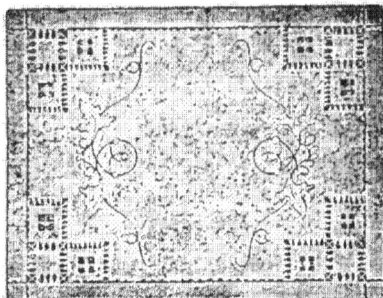

Fine hemstitched plain white linen tray cloths, with fancy open-work corners, stamped if required, sizes 18 x 27 and 20 x 30, 25c, 30c, 35c, 40c, 50c, 60c each.

Hemstitched plain white linen pillow shams, with fancy open-work corners, extra fine quality, size 32 x 32, $1.00, 1.20, 1.50, 1.75, 2.00 pair.

Hand embroidered hemstitched plain white linen pillow shams, with fancy open work in corners, in all the latest patterns, size 32 x 32, $2.25, 2.50, 2.75, 3.00, 3.50, 4.00 pair.

Hand embroidered tea cloths, with deep hemstitched double border, size 36 x 36, $2.50, 3.00, 3.50, 4.00, 6.00 each.

Hand embroidered sideboard scarfs to match, with deep hemstitched border, size 18x72, $3, 3.50, 4.00 ea.

Hand-made linen guipure lace centre pieces, size 20 x 20, $1.00, 1.25, 1.50, 1.75 each.

Linen centre pieces, with hand-made guipure linen lace edges, in following sizes : 12 x 12, 65c, 75c, 85c ; 14 x 14, 75c, 85c, $1.00 ; 20 x 20, $1.00, 1.25, 1.50 ; 36 x 36, $3.00, 3.50, 4.00, 5.00, 6.00 ; 20 x 60, $3.00, 3.50, 4.00, 5.00 each.

Satin damask doylies, with hand-made lace edges, sizes, 5 x 5, 35c ; 7 x 7, 50c ; 9 x 9, 65c ; oval shape, 9 x 13, 75c, 85c each.

Applique linen pillow shams or table covers, assorted, in all the latest designs, with fancy open-work centres and borders, size 32 x 32, 50c, 60c, 75c, 85c, $1.00, 1.25 each.

Applique linen sideboard scarfs, dresser and tray cloths, and wash stand scarfs, full range of all the newest designs procurable, sizes 20 x 36, 50c, 65c, 75c ; 20 x 54, 50c, 65c, 75c, 85c, $1.00 ; 20 x 72. 65c, 75c, 85c, $1.00, 1.25c each.

Towels.

Fine bleached huck towels, hemtitched, all pure linen, size 22 x 42, 48c pair.

German damask bleached towels, guaranteed all pure linen, in blue, gold and crimson borders, fast colors, knotted fringe, size 23 x 45, 50c pair.

Devonshire bleached huckaback towels, plain tape borders, all pure linen, sizes 20 x 40, 25c ; 22 x 43, 35c ; 23 x 46, 49c pair.

Bleached German damask towels, with heavy knotted fringe, all new designs of fancy drawn work, guaranteed all pure linen, very special, sizes 22 x 45, 50c ; 23 x 48, 65c ; 25 x 48, 75c, 85c, $1.00 pair.

Bleached linen huck towels, soft pure. finish, colored borders, fringed, all pure linen, size 21 x 42, special 35c pair.

Hemstitched damask towels, choice selection of designs, satin finish, pure linen, size 21 x 42, 50c ; 22 x 43, 65c ; 23 x 45, 75c, 85c pair.

Table Covers.

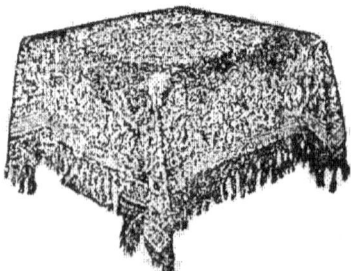

Our special satin Derby table covers, assorted, in crimson, olive, fawn, electric and brown grounds, large range of choice patterns, heavy knotted fringe, sizes 2 x 2 yds, $1.50 ; 2 x 2½, $1.75 each.

American Chenille table covers, with heavy chenille fringe, choice combination of colors, in olive, fawn, grey, crimson, electric and peacock blue, etc., sizes 1 x 1 yds, 50c, 75c ; 1¼ x 1¼ yds, 85c, $1.00 ; 1½ x 1½ yds, $1.00, 1.25 ; 2 x 2 yds, $1.75, 2.00, 2.50, 3.00 ; 2 x 2½, $3.00, 3.50, 4.00, 4.50 each.

American brocatelle table covers, assorted in crimson, fawn, myrtle, olive, electric blue, etc., richly designed, heavy deep knotted fringe, Arlington, sizes 2 x 2 yds, $1.93 ; 2 x 2½ yds, $2.75 ; Lennox, sizes 2 x 2 yds, $2.50 ; 2 x 2½ yds, $3.50 each.

Heavy English and German tapestry table covers, assorted in all the newest designs procurable, rich combination of all the latest shades, heavy knotted fringe, sizes 2 x 2 yds, $1.75, 2.00, 2.50 ; 2 x 2½ yds, $2.25, 2.50, 3.00 to 5.00 each.

White Quilts.

Fine English satin quilts, specially designed and specially finished for our trade, very choice designs, in centre pieces and scattered effects, full bleached, soft finish, size 2¼ x 2¾, or 11/4 size, $2.00, 2.25, 2.50 each.

Fine American full back toilet or Marseilles white quilts, full bleached, soft finish, beautiful designs, size 11/4, $2.00, 2.50, 3.00 each.

English Turkey chintz twilled comforters, rich Paisley designs, guaranteed fast colors, lined with colored lining, filled with cotton batting, fancy stitched, size 72 x 76, $1.50 each.

Crimson, maroon and navy blue, extra superfine all pure wool blankets, soft lofty finish, thoroughly scoured, 8 lbs, $4.80 pair.

Eiderdown Comforters.

Made up of fine French sateens, highly finished in a rare collection of rich combinations in art sateens, and thoroughly down proof, a very suitable Christmas present, size 6 x 6 feet, $5.00 ; 6 x 7 feet, $7.00 each.

Extra superfine all pure wool and extra superfine white wool blankets, thoroughly scoured, soft lofty finish, fancy borders, guaranteed full standard size and weight, 8 lbs, $3.20 pair.

Comforters, made of fine American sateens, silk finished, in rich combinations of art colors, filled with pure white cotton batting, stitched, with colored lining, these comforters weigh 5 lbs, size 72 x 76, $2.00 ; reversible, sateen on both sides, size 72 x 76, $2.50 each.

Art Sateens.

Figured sateens, consisting of all the best known English, French and American production.

Art sateens, in all colorings, large and small designs, guaranteed fast colors, 12½c, 15c, 18c, 25c, 30c, 40c.

30-inch very fine special high finished art sateens, entirely new designs, fast colors, special, 18c yd.

31-inch extra fine silk finished French sateens, exquisite and artistic designs, in all the newest combination of colorings, special, 25c yd.

31-inch finest English art sateens, choicest patterns, exceptionally rich in colorings and design, fast colors, 30c, 40c yd.

Art Denims.

Genuine printed denims, the newest in French grey, moss green, light, medium and dark blues, tan, fawn, yellow, garnet, terra cotta, etc., colored grounds, with large and small designs, now very popular for table covers, curtains, furniture coverings, draperies, cushions, etc., 36 inches wide, 30c yd.

Plain colored denims, in all colors mentioned above, 36 inches wide, 25c yd.

Fancy ticking, high art effects, with large stripes of assorted colors on yellow, olive and fawn grounds, fast colors, 32 inches, 25c yd.

Embroidered stripe printed art tickings, with combination stripes of white, blue, nile and moss green, 36 inches, 30c yd.

Art cambrics, in large checked patterns, on white and linen colored grounds, light and dark blue, cardinal, yellow, mauve, moss green bars, 32 inches, 18c yd.

Handkerchiefs, Ties, Etc.

Handkerchiefs.

Ladies' Swiss embroidered, large assortment of patterns, 9c each, or 3 for 25c ; also 10c, 12½c, 15c, 18c, or 3 for 50c.

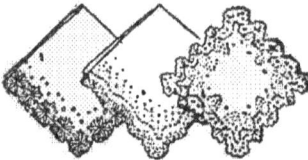

Ladies' extra fine Swiss embroidered, in all the newest patterns, 35c each, or 3 for $1.00 ; also 20c and 25c each.

Ladies' extra fine embroidered pure linen, $1.00, 1.25, 1.50, 1.75 each ; also 35c, 50c, 65c, 75c, 85c each.

Real hand-made Duchess lace, linen centres, $1.00, 1.50, 2.00, 3.00, 4.00, 5.00 each.
Real hand-made Honiton lace, linen centres, $2.00, 3.00, 4.00, 4.50, 5.50 each.

Fine Brussels point lace, linen centres, $3.75, 4.50, 5.50, to 12.00 each.

Real Maltese lace, with linen centres, $2.50 each ; also $1.00, 1.25, 1.50, 2.00 each.
Hand-made silk guipure lace, cream, silk centres, $1.00, 1.50, 2.00, 2.50 each.
Special hand-made Malta silk lace handkerchief, cream, 35c each, or 3 for $1.00.

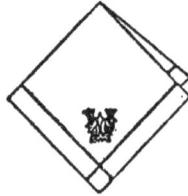

Ladies' and gents' fine pure linen, hemstitched and initialed, 25c each, or $2.75 doz.
Ladies' special pure linen, hemstitched and initialed, 20c each, or $2.25 doz.
Gents' extra fine pure Irish linen, hemstitched and initialed, 35c each, or $4.00 doz.

Letters A, B, C, D, E, F, G, H, J, K, L, M, N, P, R, S, T, W.

Plain pure Irish linen—
Ladies' hemstitched, 4 for 25c, 3 for 25c, 2 for 25c ; 15c, 18c, or 3 for 50c ; 20c, or $2.25 doz ; 25c, or $2.75 doz ; 30c, or $3.40 doz.
Gents' hemstitched, 10c, 12½c, 15c, or $1.70 doz ; 18c, or 3 for 50c ; 20c, or $2.25 doz ; 25c, or $2.75 doz ; 35c, or $4.00 doz.
Gents' tape border, 3/4 size, 4 for 25c, 3 for 25c ; 3/4 and 7/8 size, 10c, 12½c, 15c, or $1.70 doz ; 18c, or $2.00 doz ; 20c, or $2.25 doz ; 25c, or $2.75 doz ; 30c, or $3.40 doz.
Children's colored border, hemstitched Irish lawn, 15 for 25c, 10 for 25c, 8 for 25c, 6 for 25c.
Plain white hemstitched Irish lawn, 10 for 25c, 8 for 25c, 6 for 25c ; also initialed, 6 for 25c, 3 for 25c.

Gents' tape border, Irish lawn, 8 for 25c, 6 for 25c, 4 for 25c.

Small embroidered Japanese silk, colored embroidery, 5c, 9c, or 3 for 25c ; 10c, 12½c each. With embroidery and drawn work, 15c, 18c, or 3 for 50c ; 25c, 35c each.

Ladies' fine embroidered cream, 25c, 35c, 50c, 65c, 75c, $1.00 each ; also cream ground with neat colored and cream embroidery, 50c each.

Large size Japanese pure silk hemstitched and initialed handkerchiefs, 25c, 35c, or 3 for $1.00 ; 50c, and twilled, 75c each.

Ladies' and gents' plain cream, hemstitched Japanese silk, 10c, 15c, 20c, 25c, 35c, 50c, 75c, $1.00, also twill, 75c each.

Gents' black silk hemstitched Japanese, 35c, 50c, 75c each.

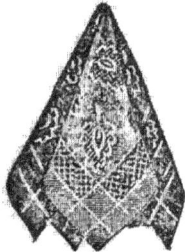

Brocaded silk handkerchiefs, cream and colored, 25c, 35c, 50c, 75c, $1.00, 1.25, 1.50 each. Black silk mufflers, 75c, $1.00, 1.25, 1.50 each. Steel grey mufflers, plaids, etc., $1.00, 1.25, 1.50, 2.25, 3.00 each. Plain cream and polka dot cashmere mufflers, 15c, 20c, 25c, 35c and 50c each.

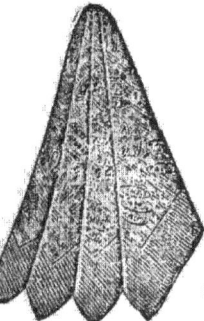

No. 1.

No. 2.

No. 1. Gents' fancy colored and cream mufflers, brocades, stripes, etc., 25c, 35c, 50c, 65c and 75c each.

No. 2. Gents' pure silk mufflers, large assortment, brocades, stripes, etc., in cream and colored, 75c, $1.00, 1.25, 1.50, 1.75, 2.00, 2.50, 3.00 and 3.50 each.

Windsor Ties.

Plain Japanese silk, hemstitched ends, in black, cream, cardinal, navy, sky, pink and heliotrope, 15c, 20c and 35c each.

Fancy pure silk plaid windsors, 20c, 25c and 30c each.

Special lines in Infants' bibs, hand and machine made, 25c, 35c and 50c ; also large range of low priced from 5c up.

Ladies' fancy ties, 1¾ yds long, in muslin and net, plain, with hem and tucks, 25c; lace trimmed, 35c each ; in pure Japanese silk, lace trimmed, 40c each.

Ladies' Pure Linen Collars and Cuffs.

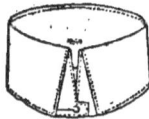 

B353.   **B354.**

B353. Ladies' high turn-down collars, 12½c.

B354. Cuffs to match, 20c, or 30c set.

B340. Narrow turn-down collars, 12½c.

B341. Cuffs to match, 20c, or 30c set.

B364. Plain stand up, also B348 plain clerical collars, 12½c each.

Plain 3-inch cuffs, 15c and 20c pair ; also special line of link cuffs, 20c pair.

B355. Nurses' turn-down collars, 18c.

B356. 3-inch turned-back cuffs to match, 25c pair.

Boys' Eton collars, B350, round corners, 15c.

B359. Deeper collar, with square corners, 18c each, or 3 for 50c.

New chiffon frillings, 15c, 25c, 35c, 45c yd.

New fancy double chiffon ruching, in all colors, 1-inch, 20c ; 1¼-inch, 25c yd.

Fancy frillings, 15c, 20c, 25c, 35c yd ; also, ostrich, in all colors, 35c yd.

Narrow cord frillings, in white and cream, 5c yd.

Chiffons, in all colors, 23-inch, 35c ; 45-inch, 65c yd.

Children's lace collars, single frill, 10c, 15c, 25c and 35c each.

Misses' and ladies' lace collars, 75c, $1.00, 1.25, 1.50 and up.

Latest novelties in veilings, 20c, 25c, 35c, 45c and 50c yd.

Sewing silk veilings, 14-inch, 20c and 25c ; 18-inch, 35c yd, in black, ivory, brown, navy and French grey.

22-inch wool barege veiling, 20c and 25c yd, in black, brown, navy and myrtle.

Infants' Shetland wool veils, 10c, 12½c, 15c, 20c, 25c and 35c each.

Infants' silk veils, 25c, 35c and 50c each.

White-wash blonde nets, suitable for ladies' ties and fancy work, 36-inch, 25c, 35c and 60c ; 72-inch, 45c and 65c yd.

Hand-made real Maltese laces, largely used for edging handkerchiefs, 25c, 35c, 50c, 75c and $1.00 yd.

Laces of all kinds in large variety, in black, white, ivory, cream and butter ; also newest combinations.

Gloves.

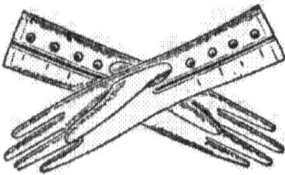

Ladies' 4-button fine French kid gloves, in tan, brown, fawn and black, special, 75c pair.

Ladies' 4-button real French kid gloves, finest quality, gusset fingers, in tan, browns, fawns, red tans and black, 90c pair.

Ladies' kid gloves, with 2 large dome fasteners, pique sewn, gusset fingers, tan, brown, fawn and black, colored embroidered backs, $1.00 pair.

Ladies' Derby kid gloves, with 4 large buttons, pique sewn, gusset fingers, Paris points, in tan, fawn, brown, ox-blood and black, $1.15 pair.

Ladies' kid gloves, "The Monarch," 2 large dome fasteners, in tan, browns, ox-blood, butter, white, pearl, grey, green mode and fawn, heavy black silk embroidered backs, pique sewn, gusset fingers, $1.49 pair.

Ladies' fine French suede gloves, with 4 large pearl buttons, gusset fingers, in tans, fawns, brown, mode and black, with fancy colored silk-stitched backs and welts to match, $1.25 pair.

Ladies' 1-clasp, fur top, wool-lined kid gloves, in tan and brown, 75c and $1.00 pair.

Ladies' 1-clasp, fur top, wool-lined mitts, in tan and brown, 75c and $1.00 pair.

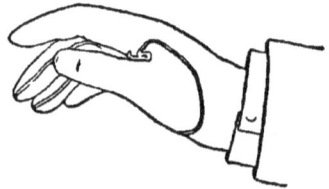

Gents' 2-clasp, unlined kid gloves, gusset fingers, in tans, fawns, browns and red tans, $1.00 pair.

Gents' 1 and 2-clasp Derby kid gloves, pique sewn, gusset fingers, in tan, browns and gold brown, guaranteed, $1.25 pair.

Men's 2-clasp, wool-lined kid gloves, in tans and brown, very special, $1.00 pair.

Men's 2-clasp, wool-lined kid gloves, pique sewn, gusset fingers, in tan and brown, $1.25 pair.

Men's 2-clasp, wool-lined, reindeer gloves, leather-bound top, gusset fingers, $1.50 pair.

Men's 2-clasp, wool-lined kid gloves, Gazelle buck, guaranteed, $2.00 pair.

Men's 2-clasp, fur-lined reindeer gloves, $2.25 pair.

Youths' 1-clasp, wool-lined kid gloves, in tan and brown, all sizes, 50c pair.

Boys' 2-clasp, wool-lined kid gloves, in tan and brown, 65c pair.

Misses' 1-clasp, fur-top, wool-lined kid gloves, in tan and brown, 69c pair.

Ladies' fancy Ringwood gloves, assorted patterns, all sizes, 25c, 35c and 45c pair.

Ladies' spun silk mitts, fancy embroidered backs, in black, 75c pair.

Ladies' plain black silk mitts, $1.00 pair.

Ladies' plain black silk mitts, fancy embroidered back, $1.05, 1.50 pair.

Hosiery.

Ladies' fine black cashmere hose, winter weight, full fashioned, double sole and heel, high spliced ankle, 3 pairs for $1.00.

Ladies' Llama black cashmere hose, high spliced heel, double sole and toe, full fashioned, fine soft finish, 50c pair.

Ladies' Indiana plain black cashmere hose, extra fine quality, double heel and toe, full fashioned, 65c, or 2 pairs for $1.25.

Ladies' fancy plaid cashmere hose, full fashioned, double sole, heel and toe, 75c pair.

Ladies' fancy embroidered cashmere hose, in all shades, with double heel, sole and toe, 35c, 50c, 65c pair.

Ladies' black open work silk hose, embroidered, in all colors, $1.25 pair.

Ladies' plain black silk hose, lace fronts, assorted patterns, $1.00 pair.

Ladies' plain black silk hose, 75c, $1.00, 1.25 pair.

Ladies' plain colored silk hose, in pinks, heliotrope, cream, white and blue, 75c pair.

Ladies' plain colored silk hose, in pink, tan, gold, blue, cream, white and cardinal, $1.00 pair.

Ladies' Lisle hose, lace fronts, assorted patterns, in black, cream and white, 50c pair.

Men's fancy plaid cashmere hose, in all shades, 50c pair.

Men's fancy embroidered cashmere hose, in blue, yellow, red, heliotrope and white, 35c, 50c pair.

Men's pure silk socks, double heel and toe, 75c pair.

Shoes.

X1. Ladies' extra choice vici kid slippers, hand-turned, flexible soles, plain or black beaded vamps, sizes 2½ to 7, $1.75.

X2. Ladies' new style fine Dongola kid 1 or 2-strap slipper, pointed toe, medium heel, very pretty, $1.50.

X3. Ladies' Melba 1-strap sandal slipper, hand-made, pointed or medium toe, splendid value, sizes 2½ to 7, $1.25.

X4. Excellent value 1-strap button slipper, opera toe, Goodyear turn, will wear well, warranted Dongola kid, sizes 2½ to 7, $1.00.

X5. Ladies' plain rubber, perfect fitting coin toe, great value, sizes 2½ to 8, 28c.

X6. Men's American black velvet slippers, worked fronts, fancy back, a comfortable, pretty slipper, sizes 6 to 11, 65c.

X6. Men's black leather opera-cut slippers, McKay-sewn, very neat and durable, sizes 6 to 11, $1.00.

X7. The old reliable Dongola kid or pebble goat, turn soles, easy on the feet, sizes 6 to 11, $1.25.

X8. Men's plain rubbers, wide soles, warranted first quality, sizes 6 to 11, 60c.

Millinery Department.

Misses' and Childrens Headwear.

No. 436. Misses' cloth tam, trimmed with narrow white braid, caught up with quills at side, braid band and buckle at side, colors green, navy brown and cardinal, 45c.

No. 391. Misses' tam, felt crown and band, brim faced with fancy checked cloth, braid rosette and two quills at side, in green, navy, brown and cardinal, 69c.

No. 554. Misses' fine felt tam, velvet band, crown handsomely

braided, scrowl patterns, caught up at side with two quills, colors brown, navy, green and cardinal, 75c.

No. 522. Misses' tam, in fancy plaid cloth, full puffed crown, velvet band, braid rosette and two quills at side, colors navy, green and red combinations, 69c.

No. 125. Child's embroidered cream Japanese silk bonnet, with fluted cape and frill, edged with lace, and inside frill of organdie, sizes 13 to 17, $1.35

No. 124. Child's cream eiderdown cap with deep cape, edged with curled China lamb trimming and fur head, sizes 13 to 17, 95c.

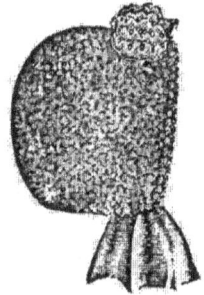

No. 117. Child's fine curled cream China lambskin cap, trimmed with fur head and lace rosettes, sizes 12 to 16, $1.50.

No. 3001. Boy's Tam o' Shanter, in heavy corded cream silk,

bow across front, and ties of same material, fine shirred crown, sizes 18 to 21, $1.50.

No. 100. Child's fine hand-made Angora hood, with swansdown ruche around front and back, in cream only, sizes for from 1 to 8 years, $1.75.

No. 135. Child's Bengaline silk poke bonnet, puffed back, poke edged with China lamb trimming, colors cream, cardinal, navy, brown and goblin, $1.50.

Black Ostrich Boas and Ruffs.

These are of Paris manufacture, from genuine Egyptian stock, perfect in color and fibre.

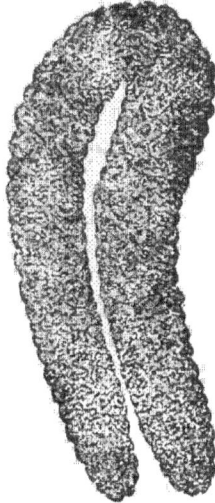

Boas, 50 in. long, $6.00, 7.50, 9.00, 12.00, 15.00.

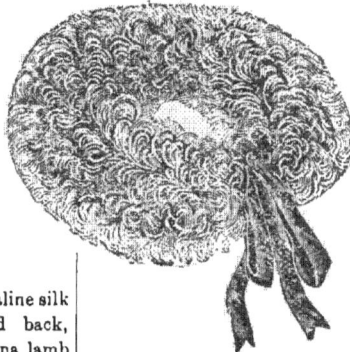

Ruffs, 18 in. long, black satin ribbon ties, $2.50, 3.00, 3.50, 4.50.

Floral Department.

These are some of the varieties most highly recommended :

Chinese sacred lilies, China grown, 5c each.

Amaryllis Johnsoni, 5 to 7 inches, 10c each.

Amaryllis Johnsoni, 7 to 9 inches, 15c each.

Hyacinths, single, unnamed, in separate colors, red, rose, white, blue and yellow, 2 for 5c.

Hyacinths, double, as above, 2 for 5.

Narcissus von zion, double, 2 for 5c.

Narcissus, paper white, 3 for 5c.

Tulips, single, mixed, 10c doz.
" double, mixed, 10c doz.
" parrot, mixed, 10c doz.

Oxalis, small size, 4 for 5c.
" large size, 2 for 5c.

Fresh supply of cut flowers received daily. All the popular varieties in season. Send for prices.

From December 18th till Christmas we will supply best South Carolina holly, large bunch 10c.

We sell South Carolina holly, as the berries on English holly will not stand the sea voyage.

Genuine English mistletoe, small bunch 10c.

We recommend the sending of all bulbs, holly, etc., by express, as they can be packed better and as they are heavy; it is as cheap as mail.

Cloaks, Waists, Shawls.

No. 2104. Ladies' beaver cloth cape, 27 inches long, colors black, navy, green, tan and brown, tubular braid trimming, with pearl buttons, $6.00.

No. 2108. Ladies' handsome cape, in fine all-wool Kersey, colors black, brown, navy and green, silk velvet collar, length 28 inches, $8.50.

No. 2002. Fur-lined cape, plain black cloth covering, grey and white squirrel lining, black Thibet or bear fur collar, fronts edged same, 30 inches long, 160 inches sweep, $25.00.

No. 2001. Fur-lined cape, plain cloth covering, colors black, green and red, hamster fur lining, black Thibet collar, fronts edged same, 30 inches long, 160 inches sweep, $20.00.

No. 2004. Fur-lined cape, fancy broche cloth covering, colors all black, and black with white, lined with grey and white squirrel, bear or Thibet fur collar, fronts edged same, length 30 inches, sweep 160 inches, $35.00.

No. 2005. Fur-lined cape, plain box-cloth covering, lined with choice all grey squirrel, solid bear collar, fronts edged same, length 30 inches, sweep 160 inches, $30.00.

No. 2006. Fur-lined cape, corded silk covering, lined with best grey squirrel, black Thibet collar, and fronts edged same, 30 inches long, 160 inches sweep, $37.50.

No. 2103. Stylish frieze cape, 28 inches long, colors black and new shades of blue, brown, fawn and green, inlaid velvet collar, $4.00.

No. 2350. Ladies' frieze capes, colors brown, green and heather mixture, straps of same material and button trimming, $5.00.

No. 1500. Misses' jackets, in black boucle curl cloth, lined black and white striped Italian, $7.50.

No. 1113. Ladies' Jackets, in choice frieze, black, fawn, green and brown, small round pearl buttons, sizes 32 to 42, $7.50

Ladies' silk sealette jackets, seal brown and black, body lined quilted satin, sleeves satin lined, sizes 32 to 42 bust, length 30 inches, $15.00, 17.50, 20.00, 22.50, 25.00.

No. 1541. Misses' jackets, beaver cloth, black, brown, navy and green, tubular braid trimmed, $6.00.

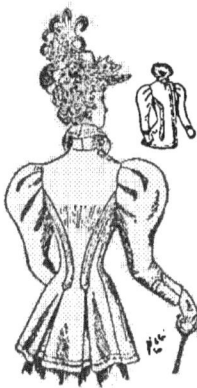

No. 1103. Ladies' Jackets, in fine Kersey cloth, black, fawn, brown, green and navy, satin lined, sizes 32 to 42, $10.00.

No. 631. Ladies' cashmere tea gown, watteau back, bishop sleeves, ribbon collar, colors black, cardinal, navy, garnet and brown, lined throughout, $3.75.

No. 642. Ladies' cashmere tea gown, colors cardinal, black, navy, garnet, peacock blue, plum and heliotrope, trimmed braid and lace, with silk ribbon ties, lined throughout, $5.00

No. 675. Ladies' English printed warm flannelette wrappers, good range of colors, including black and white, waist lined, sizes 32 to 42, $2.00.

No. 225. Ladies' waist, in fine French plaid, lined throughout, white detachable collar, sizes 32 to 38, $3.50.

No. 533. Ladies' stylish wrappers, in fine printed flannelettes, in fancy colors, trimmed with plain bands of cloth, with colored satin ribbon, waist lined, sizes 32 to 42, $2.50.

No. 325. Ladies' cashmere waists, colors black, cardinal, garnet, navy and peacock, lined all through, velvet collars and cuffs, sizes 32 to 42, $2.00.

No. 248. Ladies' new Roman stripe taffeta silk waists, fancy colors, lined all through, white linen collar, sizes 32 to 42, $6.00.

Ladies' wool eiderdown flannel dressing jackets, fly-button front, silk ribbon tie, colors cardinal, sky, grey, heliotrope, pink, tan and cream with black edging; sky, heliotrope and pink with white edging, and cream with pink edging, all sizes up to 42-inch bust, $1.39.

Ladies' wool eiderdown flannel house gowns or dressing robes, colors tan, grey, cardinal, pink, sky and heliotrope, edges bound with black silk ribbon, black wool girdle, frog fastners, small women's

sizes, 56 inches long front, women's sizes, 57 inches long front, large women's sizes, 58 inches long front, $5.50,

No. 575. Girls' frieze ulsters, colors brown, fawn, green and heather mixtures, detachable cape, with velvet collar and piping—

Length, 30, 33, 36, 39, 42, 45 in.
Price, $4.25, 4.50, 4.75, 5.00, 5.25, 5.50.

No. 576. Girls' frieze ulsters, colors brown, fawn, green and

heather mixtures, detachable cape, plain stitched cloth collar—

Length, 30, 33, 36, 39 in.
Price, $3.75, 4.00, 4.25, 4.50.
Length, 42, 45, 48, 51 in.
Price, $4.75, 5.00, 5.25, 5.50.

No. 901. Infants' long cream cashmere cloaks, silk embroidered, $1.50.

No. 903. Infants' long cream cashmere cloaks, silk embroidered, $2.00.

No. 904. Infants' long cream cashmere cloaks, silk embroidered, $2.50.

No. 906. Infants' long cream cashmere cloaks, silk embroidered, $3.00.

No. 907. Infants' long cream cashmere cloaks, silk embroidered, $3.50.

No. 908. Infants' long cream cashmere cloaks, silk embroidered, with fancy baby ribbon, $4.00.

No. 915. Infants' long cream cashmere cloaks, silk embroidered, $5.00.

No. 917. Child's wool eiderdown coat, large sailor collar, Angora fur trimmed, colors cream, tan, grey and cardinal, sizes 24, 26 and 28 inches long, $2.50.

No. 925. Child's boucle cloth coat, lined throughout, colors red and black, cadet and black, green and black mixtures, collar trimmed black Angora fur, sizes 24, 26 and 28 inches, $2.00.

No. 927. Child's boucle cloth coat, lined throughout, colors navy and brown, cadet and black, red and black mixtures, trimmed plain cloth, silk braid and small brass buttons, sizes 24, 26 and 28 inches long, $3.50.

No. 919. Child's wool eiderdown coat, circular cape, braid and Angora fur trimmed, colors cream, tan, grey and cardinal, sizes 24, 26 and 28 inches long, $3.00.

No. 921. Child's wool eiderdown coat, slashed collar, fancy braid trimmed, colors cream, tan, grey and cardinal, sizes 24, 26 and 28 inches long, $3.00.

Honeycomb shawls, colors white, grey, black, cardinal, biscuit, coral and sky, 48 x 48 inches, including fringe, 50c; 50 x 50 inches, 75c; 54 x 54 inches, $1.00; 62x62 inches, $1.25; 62x62 inches, $1.50; colors white and grey only, 65 x 65 inches, $1.75; 65 x 65 inches, $2.00.

Heavy Shawls.

Assorted colors, grey, brown and fawn, $1.50, 1.75, 2.00, 2.25, 2.50, 3.00, 3.50, 4.00, 5.00.

Wool Clouds.

Assorted shades, 25c, 35c, 50c,

Ladies' Bridal Sets.

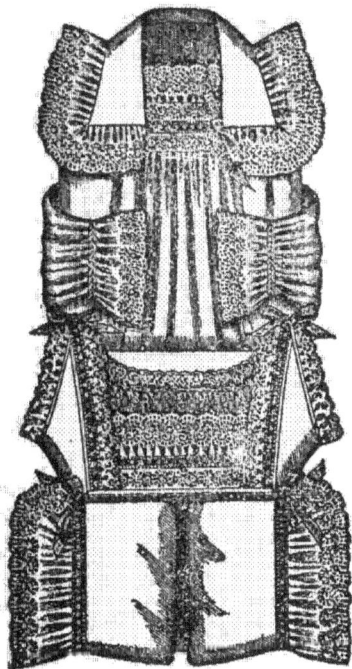

No. 1.

Comprising 4 pieces, night dress, corset cover, drawers, chemise, made of fine cambric, neatly trimmed with fine insertion and embroidery, fancy braid and ribbon, as shown in cut, $7.25.

No. 4. Child's Pinafore.

Made of lawn, Mother Hubbard style, neatly trimmed with frill of lawn and edge of embroidery.

Sizes, 1, 2, 3, 4, 5,
Ages, 1½, 3, 5, 7, 9 years.
40c each.

No. 5. Child's Pinafore.

Extra fine lawn. deep waist of tucks, fancy collar, trimmed with very fine embroidery.

Sizes, 1, 2, 3, 4,
Ages, 1½, 3, 5, 7 years.
75c each.

Sizes, 5, 6, 7, 8.
Ages, 9, 11, 12½, 14 years.
$1.00 each.

Ladies' Aprons.

No. 2.

Made of extra fine lawn, 72 inches wide, 8 inch hem, two 3-inch tucks, 40 inches long, band and sashes, 60c.

No. 3.

"The Sweet Duchess." An improved apron, by tying tapes under the band (which are attached to end of straps) to length required, an adjustment to any figure is attained, very fine lawn, neatly trimmed with embroidery, as cut, $1.00.

No. 4.   No. 5.

Men's Clothing.

Men's full dress suits, made of the very best west of England black venetian finished worsteds, unbound neat narrow silk stitched edges and lined with the best black satin, perfect cut, very latest style, all sizes, 35 to 44-inch chest measure, $19.00.

Men's Prince Albert suits, as cut, imported black unfinished worsteds and cheviots, best farmers' satin linings and trimmings, lapels faced with silk, narrow silk stitched edges, perfect fit and cut, size 35 to 44-inch chest measure, $15.00.

Men's fine west of England plain black venetian finished worsted Prince Albert suits, neatly bound with silk mohair, first-class linings and trimmings, all sizes 35 to 44-inch chest measure, $18.00.

No. 28.

Men's dark navy blue and Oxford grey beaver cloth dressing gowns, imported English goods, trimmed with silk cord and girdle to match, sizes 36 to 44-inch chest measure, $5.00.

Men's camels' hair cloth dressing gown, broken checked patterns, cardinal and fawn, also grey and fawn, diagonal weave, heavy girdle to match, warm and comfortable, $7.50.

Men's dressing gowns, fancy camels' hair cloth, best imported make, mottled patterns, fawn, green and grey dark shades, silk cord edge, trimmings and girdle to match, very stylish, $10.00.

Men's imported English camels' hair cloth dressing gowns, extra fancy all-wool cloth, in cardinal, brown and fawn mixed, mottled patterns, and fawn and brown mixtures, very best trimming to match, $15.00.

Men's house coats or smoking jackets, in fancy camels' hair cloth, fawn and grey mottled patterns, edges, pockets and cuffs neatly trimmed with cord, sizes 34 to 44-inch chest measure, $2.00.

Men's smoking jackets in Oxford grey and dark brown and fawn camels' hair cloth, cord trimming on pockets, edges and cuffs, sizes 36 to 44-inch chest measure, $4.50.

Men's fancy smoking jackets or house coats, imported English camels' hair cloth, in mid-grey, cardinal and dark fawn, diagonal and broken-checked patterns, first-class trimmings, well made, sizes 36 to 44-inch chest measure, $6.00.

Men's house coats or smoking jackets, in fawn, green and sky blue, mottled patterns, camels' hair cloth, best silk cord edges, perfect fit and cut, sizes 36 to 44-inch chest measure, $7.50.

Men's extra fancy camels' hair cloth smoking jackets or house coats, best English make, mottled patterns and broken checks, all-wool goods, green with cardinal and fawn mixtures, also light and dark fawn mixed patterns, very best trimmings to match, $10.00.

Men's corduroy vests, heavy ribbed cord, brown and drab shades, single-breasted, fly front, four pockets with flaps, well and strong made, sizes 34 to 44-inch chest measure, $1.50 each.

Men's fine English velvet corduroy vests, in drab and dark brown shades, heavy rib, four flap pockets, sizes 34 to 44-inch chest measure, $1.50 each.

Men's corduroy vests, odorless, plain and fancy cord, lined with cardinal flannel, in bronze, drab, navy blue and green, single-breasted, four flap pockets, sizes 34 to 42-inch chest measure, $2.50 each.

Men's fancy vests, silk and wool mixtures, best flannel linings, in black with red or blue spot, bronze with sky spot, navy with white, myrtle with gold, and tan with cardinal spots, latest English style, sizes 34 to 44-inch chest measure, $2.50 each.

Men's full dress vests, the latest fashionable cut, best imported plain white pique, fine cord, lined with best satin to match, sizes 36 to 40-inch chest measure, $2.00 each.

Men's full dress vests, in plain black and plain white silk, single-breasted, best satin linings, very neat and stylish, sizes 36 to 40-inch chest measures, $2.50 each.

Men's fancy full dress vests, best English make, in white with sky-blue spot, and black with heliotrope spot, neat and stylish, sizes 36 to 40-inch chest measure, $3.50 each.

Men's single-breasted fancy duck vests, with detachable pearl buttons, lined with scarlet flannel, plain drab, plain tan, and tan with green or sky-blue silk spots, sizes 34 to 42-inch chest measure, $2.50.

Men's double-breasted fancy vests, all-wool imported English cloth, flannel lined, good sateen back, in black with small red check, and black with grey check, very neat and stylish, sizes 34 to 42-inch chest measure, $3.50 each.

Men's single-breasted fancy wool knit vests, good heavy weight, in navy and black, with white silk spot, brown, with blue spot, and green with red silk spot, flannel lined, warm and comfortable, sizes 34 to 42-inch chest measure, $3.50 ea.

Men's fancy vests, all-wool imported English cloth, basket pattern, with silk spot, light-brown with green spot, and black with sky-blue spot, very latest cut and style, sizes 34 to 42-inch chest measure, $5.

Men's Furnishings.

No. 1.

No. 2.

No. 3.

No. 1. Men's fine silk neckwear, in four-in-hand shapes, choice designs and colorings, light and dark shades, 2½ inches wide by 44 inches long, satin lined, 25c, 50c. each.

No. 2. Men's fine silk and satin Lombard ties, to tie in four-in-hand or bow shape, made all round, to tie at either end, latest patterns and colorings, 25c, 35c. each.

No. 3. Men's fine silk and satin ties, puff shape, choicest Crefeld silks, newest designs and colors, latest shape, satin lined, light and dark shades, 35c, 50c each.

No. 4.

No. 4. Men's fine silk and satin bow ties, newest shapes, latest designs and colorings, satin lined, to fasten at back with elastic, fitting any size collar, light and dark shades, 25c, 35c each.

No. 5.

No. 5. Men's fine silk neckwear, in made-up knot style, latest shape, newest patterns and colorings, satin lined, 25c each.

No. 6.

No. 6. Men's fine silk neckwear, in made-up knot style, latest Crefeld silks, newest shape, best satin lined, beautiful designs and colorings, light

and dark shades, 50c, 75c each.

No. 7. Men's fine silk neckwear, in flowing end shape, to tie in small knot, with soft flowing ends, latest colorings, best Crefeld and Macclesfield silks, 50c, 75c, $1.00 each.

No. 8. Men's fine neckwear, in four-in-hand shape, very latest importations of Crefeld and Macclesfield silks, made in the newest shapes, 2¼ inches wide, 45 inches long, best silk-lined, 50c, 75c, $1.00 ea.

No. 9.

No. 9. Men's "full-dress bosom protectors," in black silk or satin, with stand-up band to protect collar, white quilted satin linings, $1.00 each.

No. 10. Men's full-dress bosom protectors, in black silk and satin, collar protector attached, light tinted silk linings, quilted as cut No. 9, $1.50 each.

Fancy Suspenders.

No. 11. Men's plain satin suspenders, silk elastic ends, fancy buckles, in black, white, pink, mauve, maroon, pale blue and old gold, $1.00 pair.

No. 12. Men's plain satin suspenders, silk elastic ends, heavy quality, fancy buckle, in black, white, pink, pale blue, mauve, maroon, drab and old gold, $1.25, 1.50 pair.

No. 13. Men's plain satin suspenders, silk embroidered,

fancy buckle, silk ends, in black, white, pink, pale blue, mauve, maroon and old gold, $1.00 pair.

No. 14. Men's fine satin suspenders, silk elastic ends, silk embroidered, kid-stayed back, in black, white, pink, pale blue, mauve, maroon, drab and old gold $1.25, 1.50 pair.

No. 15. Men's extra fine quality satin suspenders, best silk embroidered, kid-stayed back, silk elastic ends, in black, white, pink, pale blue, mauve, maroon, drab and old gold $2.00 pair.

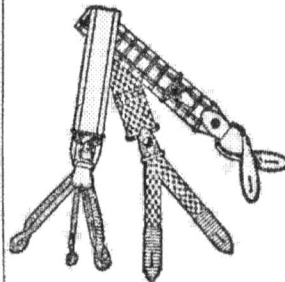

No. 16. Men's fine elastic web suspenders, silk ends and drawers supporters, double stitched, kid-stayed back, patent roll-plated buckles, light tints and white shades, guaranteed for two years, $1.50 pair.

No. 17. Men's fine leather suspenders, very soft, strong buckles, hand-sewn, all sizes, $1.00 pair.

N.B.—All satin suspenders done up one pair in box.

Half Hose.

No. 18. Men's fine cashmere half-hose, in fancy plaids and stripes, full-fashioned, double heel and toe, sizes 10, 10½, 11-inch, 50c pair.

No. 19. Men's fine wool half-hose, in fancy plaids, heavy weight, very soft finish, double heel and toe, all sizes 10 to 11-inch, $1.00 pair.

Night Robes and Pyjamas.

No. 20. Men's fine twilled cotton night robes, with fancy silk embroidered front, collar attached and pocket, large loose bodies, 54 inch long, all sizes, 14 to 19 inch collar, $1.00 each.

No. 21. Men's fine white cotton night robes, fancy silk trimmed, collar attached and pocket, light weight, well made, all sizes, 14 to 19-inch collar, $1.50 each.

No. 22. Men's extra fine white cambric night robes, best fancy silk embroidered front, best make and finish, large body, collar attached and pocket, all sizes, 14 to 19-inch collar, $2.00 each.

No. 23. Men's fine natural wool night robes, large bodies, extra long, double breast, pearl buttons, small, medium, large and extra large men's sizes, $2.00.

No. 24. Men's extra fine natural wool night robes, best English make, large long bodies, double front, pearl buttons, unshrinkable, small, medium, large and extra large men's sizes, $4.00.

No. 25. Men's fine natural wool pyjamas or sleeping suits, collar and pocket, medium weight, pearl buttons, all sizes, 34 to 46 inches chest measure, $2.50.

No. 26. Men's fine sateen pyjamas, collar and pocket, silk fasteners, light shades, all sizes, 36 to 42 inches chest measure, $3.50.

No. 27. Men's fine sateen pyjamas, collar and pocket, silk fasteners, extra well made and finished, full sizes, 36 to 42 inches chest measure, $4.50 each.

Cambric Shirts.

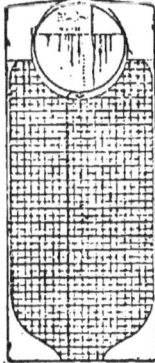

No. A. Men's fine white laundered shirts, with colored bosom and cuffs in neat pin checks, plaids and fancy patterns, open front, cuffs attached or detached, in all latest fall shades, all sizes, 14 to 17½ inch collar, 75c ea.

No. B. Men's fine colored cambric shirts, open front, separate or attached cuffs, in checks, plaids and fancy effects, newest American patterns, all sizes, 14 to 17½-inch collar, $1.00 each.

Bath Robes.

No. 28. Men's Turkish bath robes, in white with colored border, pockets, hood and girdle, small, medium and large men's sizes, $4.00 ea.

No. 29. Men's bath robes, extra fine quality, made from best Turkish material in brocaded patterns, light tints, hood and girdle, small, medium and large men's sizes, $5.00 each.

No. 30. Men's extra fine quality bath robes, best Turkish cloth, hood and girdle, in light tints with fancy stripes, latest importations, small, medium and large men's sizes, $6.00 ea.

Men's Underwear.

No. 31. Men's fine imported natural wool underwear, shirts and drawers, full fashioned, double breasted, ribbed skirt and cuffs, best trimmed, all sizes, 34 to 44 inches chest measure, $1.50 each.

No. 32. Men's fine natural wool underwear, shirt and drawers, hand made, unshrinkable, full fashioned, double breasted, pearl buttons, "spliced seats," all sizes, 34 to 44 inches chest measure, $2.00 each.

No. 33. Men's fine imported silk and wool underwear, shirts and drawers, medium weight, ribbed skirt and wrist, natural color, all sizes, 34 to 44 inches chest measure, $2.50 each.

No. 34. Men's finest imported silk and Llama wool under-shirts and drawers, double breasted, in silver grey and gold shades, heavy weight, silk trimmed, all sizes, 34 to 44 inches chest measure, $3.50 each.

No. 35. Men's fine all silk underwear shirts and drawers, light weight, silk trimmed, pearl buttons, in flesh and pale blue shades, all sizes, 34 to 42 inches chest measure, $2.50; 44 and 46 inches, $3.00 each.

Cardigan Jackets.

No. 36. Men's fine Cardigan jackets, imported make, 3 pockets, worsted finish, mohair binding, in small, medium and large men's sizes, black and brown, $2.00 and 2.50 ea.

No. 37. Men's Cardigan jackets, fine imported make, elastic finish, worsted on reverse side to keep dye from coming off, in black and brown shades, silk mohair binding, medium and large sizes, $2.75, 3.00, and 3.75.

Chamois Goods.

No. 38. Men's fine imported chamois-lined chest and back protectors, assorted sizes according to price, perforated throughout, 50c, 75c, $1.00 each.

No. 39. Men's fine imported chamois-lined vests, perfect skins, perforated throughout, pearl buttons, mohair binding, all sizes, 34 to 44 inches chest measure, $2.00 each.

No. 40. Men's fine imported chamois underwear, shirts and drawers, perforated under arms, perfect skins, mohair-bound edges, especially adapted for severe climates, all sizes, 34 to 44 inches chest measure, $5.00 each garment.

Christmas Furs.

The Boston.

Ladies' black Persian lamb caperines, made from choice selected German dyed skins, bright, glossy, medium curl, edged with Alaska sable, 12 inches deep front and back, ripple shoulders, 110-inch skirt and lined with best satin, $30 00.

The Victoria.

Ladies' Alaska sable caperines, choice natural dark full-furred skins, 12 inches deep front and back, 110-inch skirt, with ripple shoulder and best satin trimmings, $27.50.

The Amanda.

Ladies' electric seal caperines, very best quality fur, 13 inches deep, 160-inch ripple skirt, collar, fronts and skirt trimmed with imitation chinchilla, best satin linings and deep half-roll storm collar, $25.00.

The Bristol.

Ladies' and Misses' electric seal caperines, with imitation chinchilla trimming, 12 inches deep, 110-inch skirt, deep storm collar and fine satin linings, $15.00.

Ladies' Greenland seal caperines, best selected skins, 12 inches deep, 110-inch skirt, with ripple shoulder, edged with best black Thibet fur, and deep storm collar, same style as "The Bristol." $15.00.

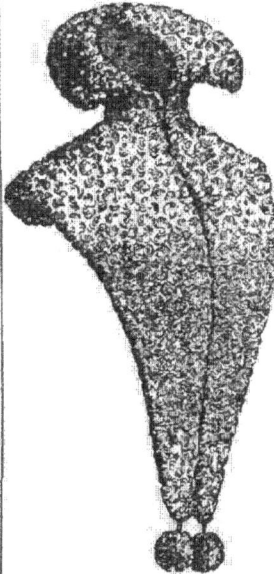

The Gloster.

Ladies' and Misses' grey lamb

caperines, large and medium light curl, good pearl grey satin linings, back 12 inches deep, high storm collar and pointed front with drops, $12.50.

The Yukon.

Ladies' extra choice Alaska sable visites, with 6-inch back, high storm collar and deep front, finished with drops, $15.00.

Ladies' Persian lamb visites, finest selected skins, medium large bright glossy curl and best satin linings, as the Yukon, $15.00.

Ladies' beaver visites, same style as the Yukon, made from the best full-furred skins only, $15.00.

Ladies' grey lamb visites, as cut, extra choice, medium light curl and best satin linings, $6.75.

The Dora.

Ladies' No. 1 quality Persian lamb, Alaska sable and beaver storm collars, with deep half-roll collar and satin linings, $12.50 each.

Ladies' grey lamb storm collars, choice skins, medium light curl, satin linings, as cut, $5.00.

Ladies' astrachan storm collars, choice bright skins, best German dye and satin linings, $4.00.

dor mink scarfs, with 2 heads
and 8 tails, 44 inches long,
$15.00.

Ladies' Alaska sable scarfs,
especially selected skins,
shaped at back, with 8 tails
and two heads, 44 inches
long, $12.50.

Ladies' Alaska sable scarfs, No.
1 quality, with 2 heads and 8
tails, $10.00.

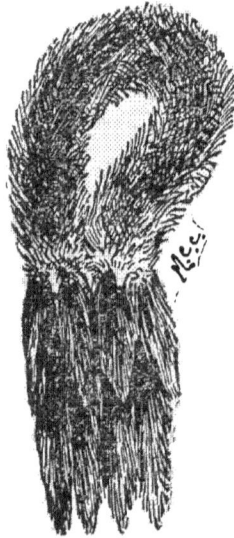

No. 1.
Ladies' extra choice Alaska
sable and dark Canadian mink
scarfs, 48 inches long, 4 heads
and 12 tails, $15.00 each

No. 4.
Ladies' dark Labrador mink
neck scarfs, choice full-furred
skins, with 2 heads and 6
tails, $10.00.
Ladies' Alaska sable scarfs, natural dark selected skins, with
4 tails only, $6.00.

No. 3.
Ladies' choice Alaska sable
scarfs, 8 tails and 2 heads, 30
inches long, $7.50.

Ladies' and misses' grey lamb
neck scarfs, medium light
curl, with 2 heads and 8 tails,
as cut No. 3, $6.50.

No. 2.
Ladies' very choice dark Labra-

No. 5.
Ladies' No. 1 quality Alaska
sable neck ruffs, straight cut,
spring head, 31 inches long,
$6.50.

No. 7.

Ladies' Labrador mink and Alaska sable ruffs, 27 inches long, spring head and claws, $5.00 each.

Ladies' black Thibet, also white Thibet ruffs, 43 inches long, with silk cord, no head, extra choice full fur, $4.00 each.

No. 14.

Ladies' extra choice Alaska seal Empire muff, the latest Parisian shape, eiderdown bedding, with fancy frills, natural head, with 3 tails on front, purse at back of head, fancy figured satin ends, as cut, $18.00.

Ladies' very dark Labrador mink Empire muff, as cut, $13.50.

Ladies' choice Alaska sable Empire muff, as cut, $13.50.

Ladies' Persian lamb Empire muff, very bright even curl, $13.50.

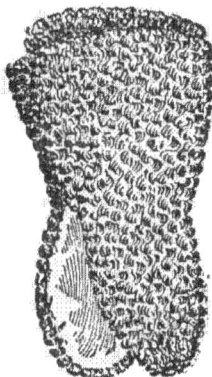

No. 13.

Ladies' Alaska seal mitts, made from prime, London dyed skins, lamb lined and calf kid faced, $15.00.

Ladies' Labrador mink mitts, very dark, natural color, $12.50.

Ladies' Alaska sable mitts, made from choice natural skins, $9.

Ladies very prime Labrador beaver mitts, fur lined, $9.00.

Ladies' Persian lamb mitts, made from choice XXX skins, very bright and even curl, $9.

Ladies' Persian lamb mitts, made from selected No. 2 skins, glossy and regular curl, $7.50.

Ladies' Persian lamb mitts, No. 3 quality, fur-lined and calf-kid faced, $6.00.

Ladies' Greenland seal mitts, lamb lined and faced with calf kid, $5.00.

Ladies' Baltic seal mitts, German dyed, $4.50.

Ladies' grey lamb mitts, extra No. 1 quality, fur lined and faced with calf kid, $4.50.

Misses' grey lamb mitts, made from selected skins, $3.50.

Ladies' black opossum mitts, fur lined, $4.00.

Ladies' Victoria opossum mitts, good dark grey color, fur lined, $4.00.

Ladies' Astrachan mitts, made from selected German dyed skins, very glossy, $4.00.

Tam o' Shanters,

Ladies' and Children's Tam o' Shanters, in grey lamb, especially selected skins, $3.75.

Ladies' and children's Iceland lamb Tam o' Shanters, pure white and satin lined, $2.50.

Men's black beaver cloth fur-lined coats, lined with dark German otter or muskrat, detachable natural hair otter collar, very dark, 50 inches long, $50.00.

Men's dark natural Labrador otter gauntlet gloves, calf kid palms and lamb lined, $25.00.

Men's medium dark natural otter gauntlet gloves, lamb lined, $20.00.

Men's Persian lamb gauntlet gloves, bright glossy German dyed skins, lamb lined, $12.50.

Men's Persian lamb gauntlet gloves, No. 2 quality, $10.00.

Men's dark Labrador beaver gauntlet gloves, lamb lined, $12.50.

Men's Labrador beaver gauntlet gloves, lamb lined, No. 2 quality, $10.00.

Men's astrachan gauntlet gloves, well lined, calf kid palms, $7.50.

Men's extra dark Canadian raccoon gauntlet mitts, buck palms, heavily lined, $5.00.

Men's wombat gauntlet mitts, dark colored skins, buck palms, heavily lined, $3.50.

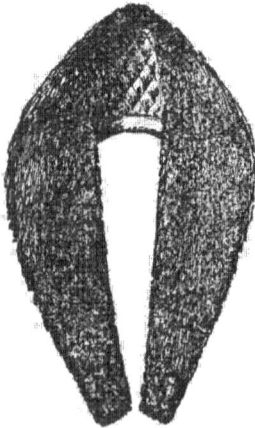

Men's detachable dark Labrador otter collar, very choicest

quality, 7 inches wide at back, quilted satin lining, $20.00.

Men's dark natural otter collars, as cut, No. 2 quality, $15.

Men's Persian lamb collar, No. 1 quality, best German dyed glossy skins, $10.50.

Men's very dark Labrador beaver collar, as cut, $10.50.

Men's astrachan collar, bright glossy curl, $4.00.

Dufferin.

Men's dark natural otter band cap, with Alaska seal crown, $15.

Wedge.

Men's choice dark natural otter wedge caps, $12.50.

Men's extra No. 1 Labrador mink wedge caps, $12.50.

Men's choice Alaska seal wedge caps, $12.50.

Men's choice dark beaver wedges, $6.50 and 7.50 each.

Dominion.

Men's choice Alaska seal, Dominion shape caps, $12.50.

Premier

Men's finest Alaska seal caps, same shape as above, $12.50.

Men's very fine Persian lamb caps, "Premier," bright full curl, $7.50.

Men's second quality Persian lamb caps, same shape as cut, $6.00.

Children's white lamb skin carriage rugs, shaped with head and tail, $3.50.

Children's White lamb skin carriage rugs, square, $2.50.

When ordering caps give style and size, state whether for man, lady, boy or child.

Grocery Department.

CHRISTMAS SPECIALS.

Prices Subject to Change.

Teas.

Our Own Importation.

We are direct importers of teas, and pay special attention to the blending of the different lines. You can save money by buying from us.

Finest indias, ceylons, congous, japans and hysons, at 15c, 20c, 25c, 35c, 50c lb.

Coffees.

We keep a full assortment of coffees, both whole and ground, which are specially roasted and ground fresh daily, put up in 1-lb. and ½-lb. cans, at 25c, 30c, 35c, 40c lb.

Dried Fruits.

We have obtained the finest fruits on the market and can guarantee you perfect satisfaction.

Currants, good clean, 6c lb; large, 7c lb.

Choice, 3 lbs for 25c; extra choice, 10c lb.

Sultana raisins, good, 9c lb; fine, 10c; choice, 12½c; extra choice, 17c lb.

Valencia raisins, fine off stalk, 7c lb.

Select layer, 3 lbs for 25c; extra select, 10c lb.

California raisins—
California muskatels, 3 lbs for 25c.
California seeded, in 1-lb packages, 2 for 25c.

Table raisins, good, 12½c lb; fine, 15c lb; choice, 20c lb; extra choice, 25c lb.

Table figs, 10c, 12½c, 15c, 17c lb.

Cooking figs, 5c lb, 6 lbs for 25c.

Evaporated apricots, very finest, 17c lb; choice, 15c; good, 12½c.

Evaporated pears, 2 lbs for 25c.

Finest golden dates, 7½c lb.

California prunes—
40 to 50 to lb, 10c lb.
60 to 70   ,,   3 lbs for 25c.
80 to 90   ,,   2   ,,   ,,   15c.
90 to 100   ,,   4   ,,   ,,   25c.

California silver prunes, 10c lb.

Crosse & Blackwell's candied peels—lemon, 15c lb; orange, 15c lb; citron, 22c lb; mixed, 18c lb.

Buchannan's candied peels — lemon, 14c lb; orange, 14c; citron, 20c; mixed, 17c lb.

Fresh Fruits in Season.

We always carry a selected stock of the best fruit on the market.

Oranges—Californias, Floridas, and Valencias.

Choice Messina lemons.

Malaga grapes.

Nuts.

When placing your order with us you can always depend on getting the very best quality, as we import the choicest and best nuts to be had.

Almonds, soft shell, 12½c lb; hard shell, 10c lb.

Brazil nuts, 15c lb.

Filberts, Sicily, 10c lb.

Pecans, large, 15c lb.

Walnuts, Grenobles, 13c lb; Marbots, 10c lb.

Shelled walnuts, Grenobles, 25c lb; shelled almonds, 25c lb.

Baking Powders.

Canadian Snowflake, 1 lb tins, 10c; 1 lb packages, 3 for 25c.

Seafoam, 1 lb tins, 2 for 25c.

Royal Standard, 1 lb tins, 15c.

Pure Gold, 3 oz tin, 10c; ½ lb tin, 13c; 6 ounce tin, 18c; 12 oz tin, 35c; 16 oz tin, 45c.

Cleveland's, small tin, 10c; ¼ lb tin, 15c; 6 oz tin, 19c; 12 oz tin, 39c; 16 oz tin, 49c.

Royal, 6 oz tin, 19c; 12 oz tin, 40c; 16 oz tin, 50c.

Dr. Price's baking powder, 6 oz tin, 19c; 12 oz tin, 38c; 2½ lb tin, $1.25.

Cooks' Friend baking powder, 19c package.

Finest baking soda, 3 lbs 10c.

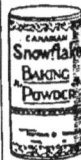

Table Jellies.

Batger's nonpareil jelly, any of the following flavors : orange, lemon, vanilla, pineapple, raspberry, strawberry, calvesfoot, noyeau and madeira—

Pints, 11c ; quarts, 20c.

Crosse & Blackwell's orange marmalade, 1 lb glass jars, 2 for 25c.

Keiller's Dundee marmalade, 1 lb pot, 18c.

Lion L. brand jams, 1 lb glass jars, 15c.

Crosse & Blackwell's jams, red currant, black currant, raspberry, strawberry, plum, 1 lb glass jars, 20c.

Crosse & Blackwell's jellies, madeira, champagne, port wine and sherry, 25c bottle, 1 lb jars.

C. & B. black currant jelly, 30c bottle.

The T. Eaton Co. jams, jellies and canned fruits—

Canned Strawberries, quarts, 30c.

Canned Raspberries, pints, 20c ; quarts, 30c.

Canned Peaches, quarts, 30c ; ½ gallons, 50c.

Canned Pears, quarts, 30c ; ½ gallons 45c.

Canned Cherries, pints, 20c ; quarts, 30c.

Jams—

Black currant, pints, 20c.

Strawberry, pints, 20c ; qts, 30c.

Raspberry, „ 20c ; „ 30c.

Gooseberry, „ 20c.

Plums, pints, 20c ; qts, 30c ; ½ gals, 45c.

Red currants, pints, 20c.

Raspberry jam pots, 10c.

Red currant jelly pots, 12½c.

Extracts.

Finest essence of lemon, vanilla, orange, clove, peppermint, wintergreen, large bottle, 10c; small bottle, 5c.

Johnston's fluid beef extracts, 2 oz pkt, 25c ; 4 oz, 45c.

Armour's, 2 oz, 25c ; 4 oz, 45c.

Johnston's fluid beef cordial, $1.00 bottle.

Sugars and Syrups.

(Prices subject to change.)

Redpath's extra standard granulated sugar, 21 lbs, $1.00.

Fine yellow sugar, 25 lbs, $1.00.

Finest icing sugar, 6c lb.

Finest powdered sugar, 6c lb.

Paris lumps, Redpath, 6½c lb.

„ „ Acadia, 6c lb.

Redpath's golden syrup, 2 lb tin, 10c.

Icings, lemon pink, white kernaline, canary, 10c pkg, $1.15 doz.

Chocolate icing, 11c pkg.

Dr. Clark's chocolate, lemon and vanilla icing, 1 lb packages, 15c.

Table Sauces and Pickles.

Lea & Perrin's Worcestershire sauce, 34c, 60c, $1.00 bottle.

Worcestershire sauce (Patterson's), 10c bot.

Holbrook sauce, 15c, 40c bottle.

Crosse & Blackwell's walnut catsup, 18c, 30c bottle.

Crosse & Blackwell's mushroom catsup, 18c, 30c bottle.

Aylmer catsup, in tins, 7½c tin.

Snider's tomato catsup, 27c bot.

Delhi „ „ 18c „

Royal salad dressing, 27c, 45c bottle.

Snider's tomato soup, 30c tin.

Colonel Skinner's mango relish, 35c bottle.

Indian mango chutney, 18c, 30c bottle.

Gillard's relish, 35c bottle.

Bengal club chutney, 18c, 30c bottle.

Capers, C. & B. 2 oz bottle, 12½c ; 4 oz, 20c (nonpareil).

Capers, C. & B. (capot), 2 oz bottle, 10c ; 4 oz, 15c.

Spanish olives, C. & B., ½ pints, 25c ; pints, 45c.

Crosse & Blackwell's pickles, pints, mixed walnuts, chow chow, gherkins and onions,

27c bottle ; the same, with patent stoppers, 30c bottle.

Half-pints, mixed walnut, chow chow, gherkins and white onions, 20c bottle.

Captain White's Oriental pickles, 30c bottle.

Horse radish, 20 oz bottle, 18c ; ½ pint bottle, 9c.

Morton's pickles, mixed white onions, chow chow and gherkins, 20c bottle.

Claxton's mixed pickles, 20 oz bottle, 2 for 25c.

Lion L. brand mixed pickles, 1 gallon pail, 45c.

C. & B. pure malt vinegar, reputed pints, 10c ; imperial pints, 15c ; reputed quarts, 20c ; imperial quart, 25c.

Biscuits.

T. B. & Conf. Co. cream sodas, 3 lb tin box, 25c ; sodas, 3 lb box, 20c.

Graham wafers, 1 lb box, 10c.

Graham wafers, 2 lb packages, 22c box.

Lemon snaps, 1 lb box, 10c.

Wine snaps, 1 lb box, 10c.

Jelly wafers, 1 lb box, 14c.

Marsh mellow, „ 15c.

Jubilee, „ 15c.

Oatmeal wafers, „ 11c.

Abernethy, „ 10c.

Vanilla crisp, „ 13c.

„ wafers, „ 15c.

Ginger nuts, „ 11c.

Molasses snaps, „ 7c.

Lemon biscuits, „ 11c.

Jam jams, „ 13c.

Almond bar, „ 15c.

Tea biscuits, „ 13c.

Arrowroot, „ 13c.

Vanilla snaps, „ 10c.

Social teas, „ 15c.

Moss wafers, „ 14c.

Household, „ 14c.

Cottage mixed, „ 10c.

Curtains and Draperies.

No. 6757. Fine Nottingham lace curtains, 54 inches wide, 3½ yards long, taped and scalloped edges, white or ecru, $1.00 pair.

No. 9479. Fine Swiss lace curtains, Irish point, 52 inches wide, 3½ yards long, in white, ivory or ecru, $4.00 a pair.

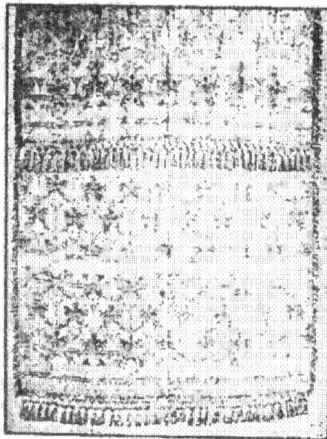

No. 820. Heavy tapestry curtains, 48 inches wide, 3 yards long, handsomely figured all over patterns, deep knotted fringe top and bottom, in combinations of gold, crimson, blue, terra cotta, rose, and nile. $3.25 pair.

No. 826. Heavy chenille portieres, 48 inches wide, 3 yards long, fringed top and bottom, fancy broken dados in crimson, terra, brown, gold, bronze, peacock, and olive, $4.50 pair.

Prices of Lace Curtains.

Nottingham and Scotch lace curtains, in white or ecru, taped edges, in a variety of new patterns, 2¾ yards long, 40c, 50c pair ; 3 yds long, 50c, 75c, $1.00 pair ; 54 inches wide, 3½ yards long, $1.00, 1.25, 1.50, 2.00 pair ; 60 inches wide, 3½ yards long, $2.00, 2.50, 3.00, 3.50, 4.00 pair.

Prices of Swiss Lace Curtains.

Swiss lace curtains, Irish point, 48 inches wide, 3½ yards long, ecru, $2.50, 2.75, 3.00 pair.

Swiss lace curtains, Irish point, 50 inches wide, 3½ yards long, white, ivory, or ecru, $3.50, 4.00, 4.50, 5.00, 5.50 pair ; 60 inches wide, 4 yards long, $6.50, 7.50, 9.00, 11.00 pair.

Prices of Tapestry Curtains.

36 inches wide, 3 yards long, all-over patterns, fringed both ends, in all full range of colors, $2.00 pair.

Tapestry curtains, 48 inches wide, 3 yards long, handsomely figured all-over patterns, deep fringe top and bottom, full range of colors, $3.00, 3.25, 3.50, 4.00, 4.50, 5.00, 6.00, 6.50, 7.00, 8.00, 10.00 pair.

Prices of Chenille Curtains.

36 inches wide, 3 yards long, in a full range of colors, fringed both ends, $2.50 pair ; 45 inches wide, $3.50, 4.00 pair ; 46 inches wide, $4.25, 4.50 pair ; 48 inches wide, $5.00, 6.00 pair.

48 inches wide, 3 yards long, all-over patterns, $6.50, 8.00, 10.00 pair.

Carpet Sweepers.

"Grand Rapids," Bissell's, cyco bearings, in assorted woods, finely finished, $2.75 each.

"Jubilee Sweeper," Bissell's, highly finished, in assorted woods, cyco bearings, dust proof, latest improvements, $3.00 each.

Bissell's celebrated Gold Medal carpet sweepers, nickel-plated, highly finished woods, dust proof, cyco bearings, $3.25 each

"Crown Jewel," Bissell's, highly finished in assorted woods, $1.50 each.

Rugs.

American moquette rugs, in a very large range of patterns and all the newest colorings, including Delft blue, green, terra cotta, wine, brown, fawn and cream ; floral, panel and Persian designs, sizes 36 x 72 inches, $3.00 ; 27 x 60 inches, $2.25 ; 18 x 36 inches, 85c each.

Best English Dag Dag or Wilton rugs, in panel patterns, with centres, in the following colors, wine, fawn and green, with floral borders, also in floral and conventional patterns, in all the latest and most effective blending of colors,

Size 36 x 63 inches, fringed ends, $6.25 each.
" 18 x 36 " " sides, 2.25 "
" 13 x 30 " " ends, 1.25 "

Heavy English Axminster rugs, in floral and conventional designs, rich dark shades, in brown, blue, terra cotta, sage and bronze, with 6-inch fringed ends, sizes 36 x 72 inches, $5.00 ; 32 x 64 inches $4.00 each.

Mohair plush rugs, fringed ends, in shades of green, old gold, crimson and brown, curled centres, sizes 30 x 64 inches $6 00 ; 36 x 72 inches, $8.00 each.

Also in door sizes, in the following shades, viz., blue, crimson, terra cotta, old gold, brown, black and green, sizes 15 x 32 inches $1.50 ; 12 x 32 inches, $1.25 ; 12 x 30, $1.15 each.

Reversible Smyrna rugs, fringed ends, in all the leading shades, a very heavy serviceable rug, sizes 36 x 72 inches $4.50; 30 x 60 inches, $3.00 ; 26 x 54 inches, $2.50 ; 21 x 45 inches, $1.75 ; 16 x 30, 90c each.

Saxony Axminster art squares, heavy soft pile, in rich blending of colors, in Persian, panel and conventional designs, light, medium and dark colors, sizes 6 ft. 8 in. x 9 ft. 8 in., $20.00 ; 7 ft. 5 in. x 10 ft. 1 in., $25.00 ; 8 ft. 9 in. x 10 ft. 7 in., $30.00 ; 9 ft. 9 in. x 12 ft. 11 in., $40.00 each.

White Down Cushions.

Covered in white cambric.

Odorless and Pure.

No. 1 QUALITY.

16 x 16 inches	-	-	$0 40 each.
18 x 18 "	-	-	0 50 "
20 x 20 "	-	-	0 75 "
22 x 22 "	-	-	0 90 "
24 x 24 "	-	-	1 15 "

FINEST QUALITY.

16 x 16 inches	-	-	$0 50 each.
18 x 18 "	-	-	0 75 "
20 x 20 "	-	-	1 10 "
22 x 22 "	-	-	1 40 "
24 x 24 "	-	-	1 75 "

We also keep these sizes in cheaper grades.

No. 103½C. Morris reclining easy chair, in oak or mahogany-finished frame, heavy English corduroy reversible cushion back, with spring seats, brass rod, back rests, $9.25 each.

No. 309½C. Sofa, mahogany finish, 41 inches long, silk tapestry upholstere l, spring seats, $13.00.

No. 166½C. Arm chair, mahogany-finished frame, fancy carved back, silk tapestry upholstered, spring seat, $8.75.

No. 10C. Roman chair, oak, curly birch or mahogany-finished frame, silk tapestry upholstered, spring seat, new design, $6.90.
No. 9C. Roman chair similar to above, but without back, both sides alike, $5.90.

No. 165½C. Tete, fancy scroll carved back mahogany-finished frame, silk tapestry upholstered, spring seat, $6.90.

No. 113C. Tete, Mahogany-finished frame, 32 inches long, silk tapestry upholstered, spring

No. 20C. Rocking chair, handsomely hand-carved back, in quarter-cut oak, curly birch, natural and mahogany finish, silk tapestry upholstered, spring seat, $7.25.
No. 22½C. Arm chair, without rockers,

No. 110C. Rocking chair, large size, in curly birch, natural and mahogany finish, silk plush or silk tapestry upholstered, spring

No. 116C. Ladies' parlor reception chair, mahogany finish, silk tapestry, spring seats, $5.90 each.

No. 257C. Rocking chair, mahogany, large size, beautifully inlaid pearl backs, solid embossed leather seats, $6.25.

No. 256½C. Rocking chair, mahogany finish, handsomely inlaid pearl backs, solid embossed leather cobbler-shaped seats, $5.00.

No. 22C. Rocking chair, in quarter-cut oak, curly birch, natural and mahogany finish, solid leather cobbler-shaped seats, special, at $1.75 each.

No. 355C. Rocking chair, in quarter-cut oak and birch, natural and mahogany finish, solid embossed leather cobbler-shaped seats, $2.75 each.

No. 254C. Rocking chair, high back, neatly carved in quarter-cut oak and mahogany finish, solid embossed leather seats, $3.25.

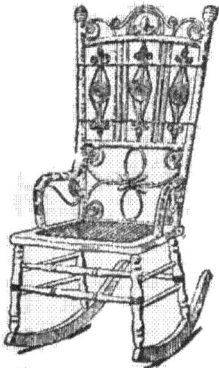

No. 1675C. Rattan rocking chairs, 16th century finish, $2.85.

No. 2½C. Misses' rocking chair, in solid oak, curly birch and mahogany patent cobbler-shaped seats, $1.25 each.

No. 1½C. Child's rocking chairs, in solid oak and imitation mahogany finish, patent cobbler-shaped seats, 95c each.

No. 2335C. Ladies' rattan rocking chair, 16th century finish, $1.00 ; reception chair to match $1.90 each.

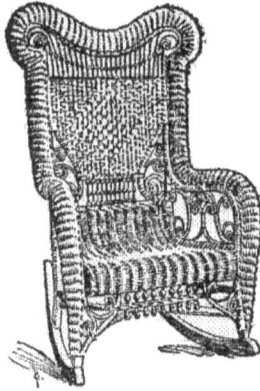

No. 2307½C. Gentleman's large size rattan rocking chair, $7.00.

No. 2305½C. Gentleman's large size rattan rocking chair, $5.00.

No. 2279½C. Rattan rocking chair, $6.75 ; reception chair to match, $6.75.

No. 2276C. Rattan reception chair, $4.65 ; rocking chair to match, $4.65.

No. 2665C. Child's high chair, rattan, with large swing table, $1.90 ; child's rocking chair to match, $1.90 each.

No. 53C. Child's writing desk, hardwood, antique finish, lid top, hinged to raise open, 20 inches wide, 16 inches deep, 26 inches high, 95c each.

No. 53½C. Youths' writing desk, ash, antique finish, lid top, 24 inches wide, 80 inches deep, 33 inches high, $1.50.

No. 60C. Youths' flat top desk, 4 drawers, top, size, 18x34 inches, height, 24 inches, $2.75 each.

No. 166½C. Fancy writing desk, made in quarter-cut oak and curly birch, mahogany finish, 30 inches wide, 60 inches high, 10 x 16 inch British bevel-plate mirror, swelled drawer fronts, shaped legs, $15.00.

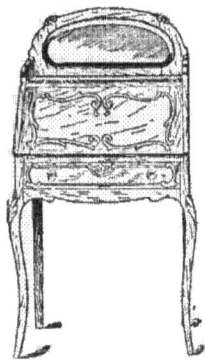

No. 8½C. Ladies' desk, made in quarter cut oak and birch, mahogany finish, 27 inches wide, 53 inches high, 8 x 22-inch bevel-plate mirror, shaped legs, neatly fitted and finished, $8.60. No. 8½. Similar to No. 8½C, without mirror, $6.75.

No. 10SC. Ladies' secretary, hardwood, antique finish, 48 inches high, 27 inches wide, fitted with pigeon holes, complete, $2.95.

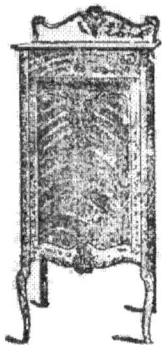

No. 140½O. Music cabinet, mahogany finish, 21 inches wide, 17 inches deep, 51 inches high, with drawer, as cut, $7.75; same, without drawer, $6.75.

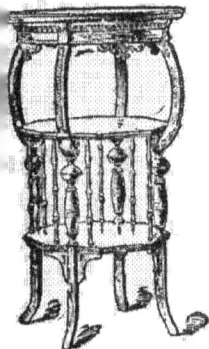

No. 221C. Parlor centre table, in quarter-cut oak, neatly carved and polished, 19 x 19 inch top, $5.75; in solid mahogany, $7.00.

No. 10C. Table, hardwood, antique finish, 16 x 16-inch top, fancy turned legs, 65c; 24 x 24-inch top, 85c; in solid oak, 20 x 20-inch top, $1.00; in solid oak, 24 x 24-inch top, $1.25.

No. 57O. Parlor centre table, in quarter-cut oak and birch, mahogany finish fancy shaped top, 25 x 27 inches, $3.65.

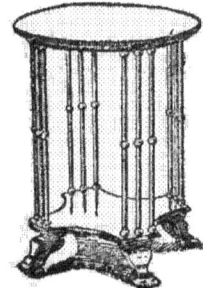

No. 110½C. Taborette, quarter-cut oak or mahogany finish, 19 inches high, 15-inch round top, $2.75 each.

No. 35½C. Parlor centre table, in quarter-cut oak and birch, mahogany finish, 27 x 27-inch top, with fancy rail, shelf, $3.00.

No. 143½O. Jardiniere stand, in quarter-cut oak and imitation mahogany, with brass feet, 19 inches high, 16 x 16 inch top, $1.65 each.

No. 15½C. Combination secretary and book-case, in solid oak and mahogany finish, 41 inches wide, 64 inches high, 12 x 14 inch plate mirror, $12.50.

No. 73½C. Combination secretary and book-case, in solid quarter-cut oak, polished, 3 ft. 7 in. wide, 6 ft. high, 12x16 in. British bevel-plate, shaped mirror, neatly hand carved and polished, $21.00.

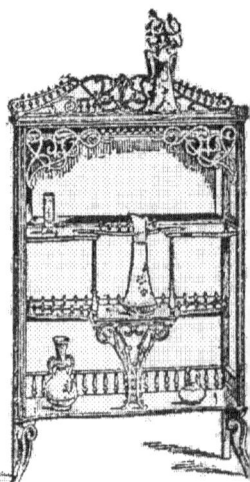

No. 138C. Parlor cabinet, in quarter-cut oak and mahogany finish, 32 in. wide, 52 in. high, 12x28 in. bevel-plate mirror, $13.00; other styles at $9.50, 11.50, 15.00, 19.00, 25.00, 30.00.

No 147½. Library table, solid quarter-cut oak, polished top, size 29 in. wide, 48 in. long, heavy turned legs, with brass claw feet and brass brackets, $13.90.

No. 85½C. Book-case, solid oak, polished, with double glass doors, moveable shelves, 40 inches wide, 72 inches high, $9.75.

No. 146C. Parlor centre table, solid mahogany, 23x23 in. shaped top, twisted legs, with brass feet and brackets, $5.50,

No. 56C. Ladies' secretary, ash, antique finish, 26 i[n.] wide, 62 in. high, fitte[d] with pigeon holes an[d] shelves, $3.95; in soli[d] oak, $4.50.

No. 57½C. Desk, similar [to] No. 56C, with large drawe[r] full width of desk, and round mirror in top, $4.75 in solid oak, $5.50.

Sewing Machines

This Department has lately been opened in connection with our Furniture Department.

All Machines are guaranteed for a period of five years. The price quoted below, with the above guarantee, speaks for itself. The workmanship is perfect; material the best, and we can confidently recommend them.

We have none of the wasteful expenses which add so much to the prices of other Machines. We can, therefore, afford to sell our Sewing Machines on the same basis of profit that we sell dry goods.

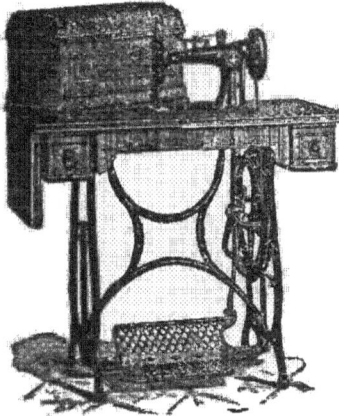

Drop Leaf, 3 Drawers,

Japanned Metal Stand,

Box Cover, Oak Woodwork,

Weight, crated, 100 lbs.

No. 1. THE LEADER, $18.50

While we guarantee **The Leader Machine** to be superior to any machine sold at anything near the price in Canada, and to be exactly as illustrated, we wish it understood that we advise every purchaser that can to order our **Improved High Arm Seamstress Machines,** as they are in every way superior to the **Leader,** and the difference in price is comparatively small.

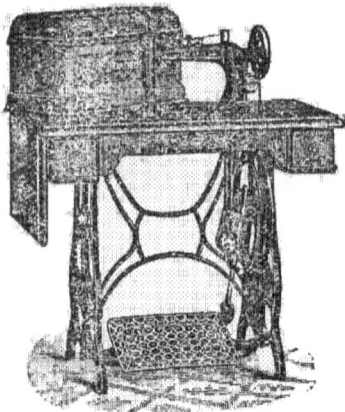

No. 3 SEAMSTRESS
3 Drawers - **$22.50**

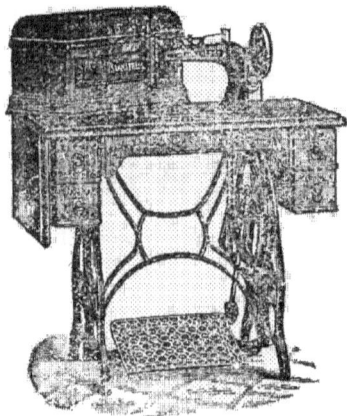

No. 4 SEAMSTRESS
5 Drawers - **$24.50**

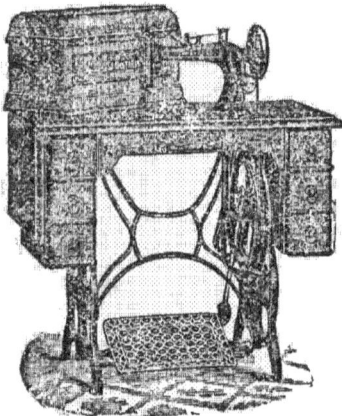

No. 5 SEAMSTRESS
7 Drawers - **$26.50**

No. 4 DROP HEAD or
CABINET TABLE SEAMSTRESS, **$29.50**

The above cuts are exact representations of our *Seamstress High Arm Sewing Machine*. The cabinet work is of the highest grade, extra well finished, made of solid oak. Bent wood work. Highly polished. Up to date in every detail. Weight, crated, 125 lbs.

SPECIAL FEATURES.

High Running. Durable. Easily Operated. Noiseless. Double Feed.
High Arm. Self-Threading Shuttle. Self-Setting Needles.
Self-Adjusting Working Parts. Automatic Bobbin Winder.
No Springs—Every movement Positive. Hardened Steel Bearings.
Rotary Shaft Movements. All Steel Attachments.

The Drop Head Case Machine is a very popular style. It is compact, simple in construction and easily handled. When machine is ready for use, the head is in the same position as on the ordinary style. When through using, it requires only one motion of the hand to drop the head down through the table completely out of sight. The machine head and attachments are the same as used on the SEAMSTRESS.

Personal instructions are not necessary. A little study of our Illustrated Instruction Book, which is supplied with each machine, will enable the most inexperienced to operate a machine successfully.

DESCRIPTION

OF THE

New High Arm "Seamstress"
Sewing Machine.

The *"Seamstress"* illustrated herein is a strictly high grade sewing machine, finished throughout in the best manner possible. It possesses all modern improvements and its mechanical construction is such that in it are combined simplicity with great strength, thus insuring ease of running, durability, and making it almost impossible for the machine to be gotten out of order.

It makes what is known as the double lock stitch, and uses two threads, which are locked together in the centre of the goods, forming a stitch which appears the same on both sides. The upper thread is drawn into position directly from the spool without passing through any holes till the eye of the needle is reached. A detailed description of the machine is as follows:

THE HEAD is handsome and pleasing in appearance, being beautifully decorated in an elaborate design worked out in gold and bright colors. All of the working parts, screws, plates, etc., are highly polished and nickel plated. The bed plate is let into the wooden table so that the surfaces of both are flush, thus greatly improving the looks of the machine, as well as facilitating the handling of the work when sewing.

THE ARM is large, very strong and well proportioned, and the clear space underneath it is 5½ by 9 inches, thus allowing the bulkiest work to be stitched and handled with ease.

THE NEEDLE is straight, has a large shank, and it is impossible to set it wrongly or for it to become fast in the bar so that it cannot be readily removed, as it is held with the latest style patent needle clamp.

THE NEEDLE BAR is round, made of hardened steel, and finely finished. It runs in hardened steel bushings, packed above and below with felt, which absorbs oil enough to lubricate the part without any danger of its running down and soiling the work.

THE TAKE UP is absolutely automatic in its action at all times and on all kinds of work.

THE AUTOMATIC BOBBIN WINDER attached to this machine is a great improvement, and with it the bobbin can be wound almost as evenly as a spool of thread, and with no care on the part of the operator except to keep the treadle moving.

THE TENSION LIBERATOR is of a new design, and enables the operator to remove the work from the machine without danger of breaking or bending the needle.

THE BEARINGS and WORKING PARTS are all hardened, carefully ground and fitted, and when kept clean and properly oiled will last a life-time.

THE HAND WHEEL is of the latest pattern and is also adjustable, so that it can be made tight or loose at will, thus enabling the operator to wind the bobbin without running the machine.

THE FEED is double, extending on both sides of the needle, is positive in its action and handles the heaviest work easily. The term "positive feed" is often used in describing other machines, but in nearly all of them it will be found that a spring is required to hold the feed bar to its bearing. The Seamstress feed motion (patented October 20th, 1891,) is free from this defect. It is so constructed that it can be raised or lowered by a simple adjustment without interfering with the feed dog. This advantage will be appreciated by all sewing machine dealers, as the old way of adjusting by set screws holding the feed dog on the feed bar has always made trouble, because, unless it was accurately done the feed dog would either strike the front or back of the needle plate, or the feed would be out of level. By the improved construction, as made by us, there is no danger of meeting with any of these difficulties. By unloosening the set screw which connects the feed push rod with the cam, and sliding it to the right or left, the feed can be adjusted as to height without displacing any of the other parts, and the feed itself will always remain perfectly level.

THE SHUTTLE is positively self-threading, of large size, cylindrical in shape, and made of the finest steel carefully hardened and beautifully polished.

THE SHUTTLE CARRIER is of a new design, and is fitted with a spring lining which balances the shuttle and does away with the noisy clicking so noticeable in other machines.

THE STAND is light and graceful, yet so proportioned as to give it great strength. It is easily kept clean and free from dust, and is furnished with oil cups to prevent soiling the floor on which it rests. The treadle and drive wheel are hung on adjustable steel centres.

THE ATTACHMENTS supplied without extra charge are of the latest design, interchangeable, and constructed to slip on the presser bar. They are made throughout of the best steel, polished and nickel plated, and there is not a particle of brass or other soft metal or a single soldered joint about them. They consist of Ruffler, Tucker, Binder, Braider Foot, Under Braider Slide Plate, Shirring Side Plate, Four Hemmers of assorted widths, Quilter, Thread Cutter, Foot Hemmer and Feller.

THE ACCESSORIES include twelve Needles, six Bobbins, Oil Can filled with oil, large and small Screw Drivers, Sewing Guide, Guide Screw, Certificate of Warranty good for five years, and elaborately illustrated Instruction Book.

ᵀᴴᴱ T. EATON C⁰·LIMITED

190 Yonge Street,   TORONTO, CAN.

INDEX.

www.ingramcontent.com/pod-product-compliance
Lightning Source LLC
Chambersburg PA
CBHW021525270326
41930CB00008B/1100